Book 2

# 30 days to more powerful intercessory prayer

Joe Engelkemier

**Pacific Press® Publishing Association**
**Nampa, Idaho**
Oshawa, Ontario, Canada

Edited by Jerry Thomas
Designed by Michelle C. Petz



ISBN 0-8163-1834-4

01 02 03 04 • 4 3 2 1

# Table of Contents
## Intercession for Others
## A 30-Day Plan


Introduction: Eager for "Something Big" .......... 5

**I. Getting Started**

1. **Pray** for God's Spirit .......... 9
2. **Make** Praying for Rain a Top Priority .......... 13
3. **Start** Everything With Prayer .......... 18
4. **Embrace** Family Prayer .......... 21
5. **Regard** Midweek a Hundred-Dollar Event .......... 25
6. **Cling** to Christ's Worthiness .......... 29
7. **Call** for Angels to Help .......... 34

**II. Private Intercession**

8. **Watch** Jesus in Prayer .......... 38
9. **Praise** God for His Mercy .......... 42
10. **Welcome** Farmer God's Pruning .......... 45
11. **Begin** a Prayer Ministry .......... 48
12. **Seek** Spirit-Filled Living .......... 53
13. **Use** the Bible as a Sword .......... 56
14. **Energize** Your Health .......... 59

**III. Group and Midweek Prayers**

15. **Urge** Principles God Gave .......... 63

16. **Start** With Telephone or Email ........ 71
17. **Ask** Forgiveness for All ........ 74
18. **Pray** Jabez Prayers (For Yourself and Others) ........ 77
19. **Show Up** Eagerly at Midweek Services ........ 81
20. **Treasure** Repentance and Revival ........ 85
21. **Practice** Preventive Praying ........ 89

**IV. For Parents, Pastors, Leaders**

22. **Flood** Heaven With Thanksgiving ........ 93
23. **Make** Your Home a Small Group ........ 97
24. **Use** Bible Biographies ........ 101
25. **Teach** From Nature ........ 105
26. **Use** Lots of Stories ........ 109
27. **Exhibit** Clarity and Enthusiasm ........ 111
28. **Encourage** Prayer Groups ........ 117

**V. Glancing Ahead**

29. **Seek** More and More of God's Spirit ........ 122
30. **Pray** "More and More" Like Jesus ........ 125

# Introduction: Eager for "Something Big"

**" ' "Call to Me, and I will answer you, and show you great and mighty things, which you [have not yet seen]" ' "**
**(Jeremiah 33:3).***

During the November 2000 elections in America, one contestant said that he sensed that "something big" would soon take place.

As you listen to or watch the news, do you get a similar feeling? The politician hoped he could unseat an incumbent. But for this whole planet could the "something big"—something truly big—be the return of Christ?

But before Jesus returns doesn't another "something big" need to take place? Isn't that getting the gospel of Revelation 14 out "to every nation, tribe, tongue, and people" (Revelation 14:6)? Doesn't that also involve our prayers for the latter rain? During Bible times, an early rain at planting time sprouted the seed and gave crops a good start. A latter rain at harvest time filled out the grain. For us today, the final latter rain will take the gospel of Revelation 14 to every community on earth.

This book deals with our need for a new thirst for the kind of intercessory prayer that will pave the way for the latter rain. The pages that follow contain suggestions about how to build more such prayer into our schedules, both privately and as congregations.

At times I cite ideas from several sources, foremost of which is the Spirit of Prophecy. This morning I re-read Ephesians 4, and I thank God that when Jesus ascended on high, He " 'gave gifts to men' " (Ephesians 4:8). Verse 11 lists these gifts: apostles, prophets, evangelists, pastors, teachers. We no longer call anyone "apostles"—people sent—but I see a missionary as a parallel. The New Testament repeatedly mentions another gift sometimes not expected, that of prophecy. In Revelation 12, that's one of the identifying marks of the remnant. Paul tells the reasons for all the gifts:

- to equip the saints for the work of ministry
- to edify the body of Christ

Ellen White considered her writings to be a "lesser light" intended to lead people to the "greater light" (*Colporteur Ministry,* 125). In my own use of the "lesser light" writings—whether full books, or compilations like *Messages to Young People*—this gift does two things for my Bible study:

- gives insights to Scripture passages I hadn't seen
- helps me apply Bible truths to daily life

Along with Spirit of Prophecy writings, I cite ideas from Andrew Murray's *The Ministry of Intercession,* Wesley Duewel's *Mighty Prevailing Prayer,* and other sources.

Murray, a contemporary of various Seventh-day Adventist pioneers, directs us to this statement of the apostles: " 'We will give ourselves continually to prayer and to the ministry of the word' " (Acts 6:4). He then points out:"Where there is much prayer there will be much of the Spirit, and where there is much of the Spirit there will be much prayer" (18). "Between our Impotence and God's Omnipotence," he wrote, "intercession is the blessed link" (25).

This movement needs tens of thousands such links! We need a grass roots thirst for more and more intercession—prayer that includes church officers, young adults, pastors, *and even children.*

For a moment consider the difference between *petition* and *intercession.* In *The Hour That Changes the World,* Dick Eastman defines *petition* as "that aspect of prayer given over to asking God for personal things" (87). Examples include school funds for a child, tuition for yourself, a personal health need, or for God's blessing upon a family need such as transportation. Petitions should never be depreciated, for out of answered petitions God leads one into the next height of prayer splendor: the fervent intercession that ultimately brings the latter rain.

*Intercession* goes to God with group needs. In its simplest form it may be for several people who need conversion. *Intercede* means "to plead or make a request in behalf of another or others." It could be a plea for God's Spirit for an entire school, a hospital, or perhaps a state or country or continent. The account in Acts 1—120 people meeting in an upper room to plead for the Holy Spirit—involved group intercession.

**An announcement that would startle?**

What would you think if your pastor made this announcement next Sabbath?

From now on, what happens on prayer meeting night will be the gauge by which we judge the success or failure of our church in this community.

On his first Sunday at the New York Tabernacle Church (Assembly of God), Pastor Jim Cymbala found that only twenty people attended. At his first prayer meeting, only two people came. A year later he made an announcement similar to the above, and followed through with that emphasis. Chapter 5 tells the results.

During the four years before I retired, I pastored two churches within twenty-five miles of Andrews University. One had an active Sabbath attendance of one hundred fifty and the other about eighty. But at both churches we seldom got a midweek attendance of more than 10 to 15 percent.

What could I have done differently? All of us need to ask, "With the midweek service being the time to especially pray for the descent of the Holy Spirit, do we have any right to expect that glorious climax if most of us aren't even there?"

I have tried to locate key Bible examples, and have researched Spirit of Prophecy comments. I share a little in almost every chapter, with a summary review in chapter 15.

This book has a three-fold purpose:

- to review what makes prayer effective
- to encourage more private intercession
- to suggest how group intercession can be more enjoyable and more effective and *better attended.*

To all God says: " ' "Call to Me, and I will answer you, and show you great and mighty things, which you [have not yet seen]" ' " (Jeremiah 33:3).

* Unless otherwise indicated, all Bible quotations are from the New King James Version

# 1

# Pray for God's Spirit

**" 'Ask and you'll get; Seek, and you'll find; Knock and the door will open' " (Luke 11:9, *The Message*).**

In this context Jesus said, "If you then, being evil, know how to give good gifts to your children, how much more will your Father in heaven give the Holy Spirit to those who ask Him?"

Our current situation?

• Prayer of any kind appears to have become more a profession than a practice.

Long before TV became society's addiction, H. M. S. Richards—founder of the Voice of Prophecy—called prayer "the most talked about and least practiced of all Christian beliefs." He apparently spoke of Christians as a whole. But *now?* Does that also describe Seventh-day Adventists?

• In most Adventist churches, only a few attend the mid-week prayer meeting.

The few tend to be older folk. Group praying, when it occurs, generally involves going around a circle, and too often wearies more than it refreshes.

**Youth needed**

"Don't let anyone think little of you because you are young," Paul wrote to a young adult. "Be their ideal; let them follow the way you teach and live; be a pattern for them in your love, your faith, and your clean thoughts" (1 Timothy 4:12, TLB). *Messages to Young People* declares: "God calls for youthful vigor, zeal, and courage. . . .

To plan with clear mind and execute with courageous hand demands fresh, uncrippled energies" (20). As Prayer Conferences have repeatedly illustrated, those "fresh, uncrippled energies" can give a power-filled thrust when it comes to fervent and non-tedious prayer and to enthusiastic Bible study. (In my book *30 Days to a More Powerful Prayer Life,* see the chapter entitled "A Spirit of Intercession").

The above paragraph about youthful vigor continues: "Young men and women are invited to give God the strength of their youth, that through the exercise of their powers, through keen thought and vigorous action, they may bring glory to Him and salvation to their fellow men" (ibid.).

*Keen thought and vigorous action!* On Christian college and academy campuses very few youth attend prayer meetings. It's partly a lack of interest, partly because of dorm worships, and partly because of required classes and labs on prayer-meeting night. Could evening labs or classes become one of the barriers that evil uses to keep students and teachers alike from attending?

Shortly after writing the above, I opened to Psalm 94, and my eyes fell upon this: "Shall the throne of iniquity, which devises evil by law, have fellowship with You?" (v. 20).

What can be done about required classes or labs that keep students from attending? I ask because at Andrews University, as I urge students to come to the mid-week service, they often reply, "I can't; I have a class at that time."

And for all of us, what about those priorities—a lawn to cut, a time for gardening, a TV program to watch—that keep up to 90 percent of an adult congregation away from the mid-week service?

**Youth as a pattern**

*"Be a pattern for them."* Where do we most need that youthful pattern? Could youth—academy, college and university, other young adults—add strength on prayer-meeting night? I saw two examples of keen thought and vigorous action this week:

- The mid-week service at Andrews University's PMC (Pioneer Memorial Church) ended with three prayers. The first two, by older men, used preachy terms. The third prayer, by a young woman, lasted less than a minute, and brought true refreshment to listeners.
- On Sabbath, a young adult had the pastoral prayer. She included everything expected in a pastoral prayer—thanksgiving, a request for two who were ill, for forgiveness, and for the speaker—yet lasted no more than 90 seconds.

How about a few words of approval for what these young adults did?

> Christ impressed upon His disciples the idea that their prayers should be short, expressing just what they wanted, and no more. He gives the length and substance [sample content] of their prayers, expressing their

desires for temporal and spiritual blessings, and their gratitude for the same. How comprehensive this sample prayer! . . . One or two minutes is long enough for any ordinary prayer" (*Testimonies for the Church,* 2: 581).

"You can do more than pray after you have prayed," an unknown Christian stated, "but you can never do more than pray until you have prayed." After suggesting that "prayer is omnipotent" the same person declared: "It can do anything God can do!"

"Anything God has done in the past," said Wesley L. Duewel, "He is able to duplicate or exceed" (*Mighty Prevailing Prayer,* 12). "While He reserves the sovereign right to work independently," he added, "His normal plan is to work in cooperation with and through the prayer and obedience of His own" (ibid.).

**"Part of God's plan"**

In the words of E. M. Bounds, "It (prayer) brings to pass things which would never otherwise occur." Ellen White put this truth simply: "It is part of God's plan to grant us, in answer to the prayer of faith, that which He would not bestow did we not thus ask" (*The Great Controversy,* 525).

What might be the result if thousands of believers would use those ideas many times a day? Isn't it time for the book of remembrance (Malachi 3:16) to be filled with hundreds and thousands of such requests? Let's never forget the latter rain promises of Zechariah 10: "Ask the Lord for rain in the time of the latter rain. The Lord will make flashing clouds; He will give them showers of rain" (v. 1).

**More about rain**

The "latter rain" can be expected just before Jesus returns. The following prophecy will again be fulfilled:

> "And it shall come to pass afterward that I will pour out My Spirit on all flesh; your sons and your daughters shall prophesy, your old men shall dream dreams, your young men shall see visions. And also on My menservants and on My maidservants I will pour out My Spirit in those days" (Joel 2:28, 29).

Note a comment made more than a hundred years ago:

> The descent of the Holy Spirit upon the church is looked forward to as in the future; but it is the privilege of the church to have it now. Seek for it, pray for it, believe for it. We must have it, and Heaven is waiting to bestow it (*Evangelism,* 701).

At that time conversions will take place with a rapidity similar to what happened in the opening chapters of Acts. Thousands will accept the gospel. Many of these new believers will almost immediately go to work sharing what they have discovered.

*Seek for it, pray for it, believe for it.* How does one do that? We will explore that topic in the next chapter.

**One more thing**

As part of this first chapter, let's get something straight: Seventh-day Adventists cannot think of themselves as "just another denomination." From the first, it has been a *movement*—a movement foretold in Revelation 12 and 14. No other group on earth comes close to the two identifying characteristics of Revelation 12: keeping *all ten* of the Ten Commandments, and possession of the prophetic gift. Still less does any group come close to the eight additional identifying marks of Revelation 14!

The God-chosen instrument of the prophetic gift has written much about the latter rain—insights that deal with Joel 2, Zechariah 10, and other passages. We focus on several really striking insights in the next chapter.

This is a repeat statement:

> " ' "Call to Me, and I will answer you, and show you great and mighty things, which you [have not yet seen]" ' " (Jeremiah 33:3).

**Applications**

- Why not memorize the opening text and the following? "It is part of God's plan to grant us, in answer to the prayer of faith, that which He would not bestow did we not thus ask" (*The Great Controversy,* 525). Then keep both before God as a reason for Him to act.
- From this chapter select what you see as the most striking new idea, write it on a 3-by-5 card, keep it with you and silently pray about it as you come and go.

# 2

# Make Praying for Rain a Top Priority

**"Ask the Lord for rain in the time of the latter rain. The Lord will make flashing clouds; He will give them showers of rain" (Zechariah 10:1).**

**"Buildings burning as if they were made of pitch."** Would something like that as a headline tomorrow morning get your attention?

"In the last days the times will be full of danger," Paul warned (2 Timothy 3:1, Phillips) May I refer to volume 9 of *Testimonies for the Church*? The opening chapter, "The Final Crisis," includes statements such as these:

> The Spirit of God is gradually but surely being withdrawn from the earth (11).
>
> Great changes are soon to take place in the world, and the final movements will be rapid ones (ibid.).
>
> On one occasion, when in New York City, I was in the night season called upon to behold buildings rising story after story toward heaven. . . . The scene that next passed before me was an alarm of fire. Men looked at the lofty and supposedly fire-proof buildings and said, "They are perfectly safe." But these buildings were consumed as if made of pitch. The fire engines could do nothing to stay the destruction (ibid., 12, 13).

Suppose tonight's ten o'clock news showed buildings in New York—or London—burning that way. Will God need to bring about that kind of "whatever it takes" attention-getter before we really pray for the latter rain?

I don't find anything in the context of the above that suggests any kind of atomic explosion. But whatever it is, will your pastor need to urge midweek attendance? Will a reminder from the pulpit be enough? Don't we need a grass-roots movement in every congregation? Don't just attend; take another family with you. Then urge them to do the same the following week.

Avoid fear tactics. But at churches both small and large, the pastor or whoever leads out for midweek meetings could hand out copies or read from the first two or three pages of "The Final Crisis" and discuss it with what hopefully will be a fuller house at the next prayer meeting. If you separate into small groups for seasons of earnest prayer, why not especially pray for God's Spirit to hasten the latter rain?

According to the *SDA Yearbook,* this denomination has more than 40,000 churches. As of the 2000 General Conference, world membership passed eleven million. If even a third of these attended prayer meeting, what an impact their prayers could make!

What would it take to awaken a spirit of intercession such as pictured in the following words?

> A revival of true godliness among us is the greatest and most urgent of all our needs. To seek this should be our first work. . . . Our heavenly Father is more willing to give His Holy Spirit to them that ask Him, than are earthly parents to give good gifts to their children.
>
> But it is our work, by confession, humiliation, repentance, and earnest prayer, to fulfill the conditions upon which God has promised to grant us His blessing. A revival need be expected only in answer to prayer (*Selected Messages,* 1:121).

**A sneak attack**

As I pen these words (late October of 2000) the October 23 issue of *Newsweek* has published "A Sneak Attack." It describes the loss of seventeen American sailors when terrorist bombers blasted the Navy destroyer *Cole* at a Yemen harbor. The report included these words:

"*Cole* Cmdr. Kirk Lippold . . . was planning to tether to a buoy for just a few hours, long enough to 'gas and go,' before pressing on toward the Persian Gulf . . . Nobody aboard the *Cole,* certainly, was expecting to die in the 95-degree heat of that shimmering new day.

"The two sailors aboard a 20-foot fiberglass vessel puttering nearby, however, probably had very specific plans to die . . . At about 9:45 a.m., according to fleet officers, as the smaller boat glided along the destroyer's port side, the two men apparently detonated an enormous load of explosives" (27).

The same issue of *Newsweek* discussed the renewed violence in the Middle

East. The chief peace negotiator for the Palestinians, Saeb Erekat, predicted: "It's going to be a killing field out there. The worst is yet to come" (ibid., 32). "One thing is certain," said *Newsweek*, "what was a rather narrow struggle between Palestinians and Israelis a few weeks ago, had, by this week, rippled far beyond."

*Newsweek* noted rapid changes taking place. We can never use political, military, or economic developments as a basis for what to expect, but we can say two things:

- "The final movements will be rapid ones" (*Testimonies*, 9:11).
- While God has blessed this end-time movement beyond all expectations, we need the Holy Spirit now more than at any time in history.

**Do prayers for the Spirit do any good?**

Most of us are aware of the prophecy in Revelation 18:1 that as time closes another angel (message) will go forth with "great authority." The angel speaks with a "loud voice" (v. 2). This message is a result of the latter rain. But do we ever pray—alone or in a group—for the outpouring of the Holy Spirit? And if we do, do such prayers do any good?

Jesus urged us to pray for the Holy Spirit (Luke 11:9). We can expect this final message to be attended with the greatest demonstration of God's saving power in all history. Isaiah 60, which parallels Revelation 18, includes this prediction: "Darkness shall cover the earth, and deep darkness the people; but the Lord will arise over you, and His glory will be seen upon you. The Gentiles shall come to your light, and kings to the brightness of your rising" (vs. 2, 3). When God's people so fully separate themselves from evil that the light of heaven can rest upon them in full measure, thousands will be converted. The next section contains an abbreviated summary of statements I cited.

**Light everywhere!**

"When divine power is combined with human effort, the work will spread like fire in the stubble. . . . Angels will do a work which men might have had the blessing of accomplishing, had they not neglected to answer the claims of God" (*Selected Messages*, 1:118).

"There will be a series of events revealing that God is master of the situation. . . . Through most wonderful workings of divine providence, mountains of difficulty will be removed and cast into the sea. The message that means so much to the dwellers upon the earth will be heard and understood" (*Testimonies*, 9:96).

"The ranks will not be diminished. Those who are firm and true will close up the vacancies that are made by those who become offended and apostatize" (*Manuscript Releases*, 2:57).

"Light will be communicated to every city and town. The earth will be filled with the knowledge of salvation" (*Evangelism,* 694).

For emphasis let me repeat four "coming events":

- "The work will spread like fire in the stubble. . . . Angels will do a work which men might have had the blessing of accomplishing."
- "Through the most wonderful workings of divine providence, mountains of difficulty will be removed and cast into the sea."
- "The ranks will not be diminished."
- "Light will be communicated to every city and town. The earth will be filled with the knowledge of salvation."

**"You can change history"**

The months ahead will see a lot of the unexpected. Your prayers—both at home and at prayer meeting—will really count! They could even change the course of history!

Back in 1938, Jewish businesses and synagogues all across Germany were attacked in a Nazi-orchestrated campaign, with many Jews sent to concentration camps. Sixty-two years later, in early November of 2000, more than 200,000 German citizens, led by Chancellor Gerhard Schroeder, solemnly marched through Berlin in what a South Bend *Tribune* headline called a "rally against hate"—intended to protest rising neo-Nazi violence.

This coincided with the opening of Germany's first rabbinical school since the Holocaust. At that opening, the leader of Germany's Jewish community told of a German police officer who in 1938 prevented Nazi storm troopers from touching a synagogue on that site. He then said, "This example teaches us. By standing together, by not looking away, you can change history" (ibid.).

*You can change history!* Long before the above reference to a 1938 German police officer, a German leader named Martin Luther went to his knees in behalf of the Protestant Reformation. His prayers changed history, for "from the secret place of prayer came the power that shook the world in the Great Reformation" (*The Great Controversy,* 210).

Your faithful prayers, at home as well as at prayer meeting, can help bring about the events described here:

The revenue of glory has been accumulating for this closing work of the third angel's message. Of the prayers that have been ascending for the fulfillment of the promise—the descent of the Holy Spirit—not one has been lost. Each prayer has been accumulating, ready to overflow and pour forth a healing flood of heavenly influence and accumulated light all over the world (*Manuscript Releases,* volume 21:155).

*Not one prayer has been lost!* Do you see why every prayer-meeting night should include prayers for the descent of the Holy Spirit? Do you see why your prayers "can change history"?

**Application**

- Commit to memory: "Of the prayers that have been ascending for the descent of the Holy Spirit, not one has been lost."
- At the start of 2000 Dwight Nelson, NET '98 speaker, did a series at the Andrews church called "The Second Coming of the Holy Spirit." What do you like most about thinking of the latter rain that way?

# 3

# Start Everything With Prayer

**"Every morning I lay out the pieces of my life on your altar" (Psalm 5:3, *The Message*).**

In your imagination picture yourself in a situation in which a reduction of oxygen made death imminent.

"There are 23 of us here," wrote Lt. Capt. Dmitry Kolesnikov, after a shattering explosion sank the Russian submarine *Kursk* on August 12, 2000. As he wrote, the lights dimmed, the temperature dropped, water leaked in, and the air became increasingly foul. The explosion had killed most of the 118-man crew immediately, but where he ended up, Kolesnikov scribbled a few words. In a note written as breathing became difficult, he said, "All the crew from the sixth, seventh, and eighth compartments went over to the ninth. . . . We made this decision as a result of the accident. None of us can get to the surface."

According to *Newsweek,* "the note began with neat cursive handwriting, suggesting the lights were still on. It included a message for Kolesnikov's wife Olga, whom he had married only three months before" (6 November 2000, 43). On the back of the paper the writing was smudged, nearly illegible. "By then," *Newsweek* said, "apparently the lights had gone out for good. 'I am writing blind,' Kolesnikov scribbled. Then he wrapped the letter in plastic and put it in his pocket, where it was found after a Russian diver recovered his body and three others from the *Kursk*" (ibid., 43, 44).

Can you imagine dying that way?

### The preciousness of oxygen

Webster defines oxygen as a gaseous chemical element that makes up approximately one-fifth of the atmosphere. Very active, it combines with nearly all other elements, and is essential to life processes. Without it, as aboard the *Kursk,* death is certain.

Consider this definition of a spiritual parallel: "Prayer is the breath of the soul. It is the secret of spiritual power" (*Messages to Young People,* 249). "Neglect the exercise of prayer, or engage in prayer spasmodically, now and then, as seems convenient," the same author declares, "and you lose your hold on God. The spiritual faculties lose their vitality, the religious experience lacks health and vigor" (ibid., 249, 250).

A prelude to death? An eventual death in the lake of fire?

It appears that the secular world begins new days with no thought of God. Could that be true for large parts of the Christian community? How about in Seventh-day Adventist homes? As you awaken in the morning do your first thoughts fasten on Jesus? Do feelings similar to this chapter's opening verse grip you?

For the first dozen years I taught the class Workshop in Prayer at Andrews University, we used the devotional book *My Life Today.* Comments for this chapter's first verse, for January 11, included:

> The very first outbreathing of the soul in the morning should be for the presence of Jesus. "Without Me," He says, "you can do nothing." . . . We need Him every hour. And we should pray in the morning that as the sun illuminates the landscape, and fills the world with light, so the Sun of Righteousness may shine into the chambers of mind and heart, and make us all light in the Lord (15).

Doesn't the above *outbreathing* come from the word *breath?* The same devotional contains this suggestion: "Let your prayer be, 'Take me, O Lord, as wholly Thine. I lay all my plans at Thy feet. Use me today in Thy service. Abide with me, and let all my work be wrought in Thee.' This is a daily matter" (ibid., 6).

**Incredible blessings**

The blessings from that type of bedside prayer habit cannot be put into words! Here's one mentioned on the same page: "The surrender of all our powers to God greatly simplifies the problem of life. It weakens and cuts short a thousand struggles with the passions of the natural heart" (ibid.).

Surrender doesn't just *simplify.* It *greatly* simplifies. And that's not all. That lifestyle becomes "a golden cord that binds the souls of both youth and aged to Christ. Through it the willing and obedient are brought safely through dark and intricate paths to the city of God" (ibid.). What sensible person doesn't want these benefits?

- life greatly simplified
- struggles with carnal thoughts cut short

- safe passage through dark paths
- entrance to city of God

A billion dollars could never purchase these treasures! But their cost? *Starting the day with a bedside surrender to Jesus!* The above bedside outreach can lead into a day filled with much prayer: Thank-You sentences, thought prayers, grace at the table, family worship praises, guidance requests, varied petitions, intercession, etc. See chapter 11 for a discussion of Paul's "pray without ceasing" (1 Thessalonians 5:17).

**Application**

- "There is no limit to the good you may do" (*My Life Today,* 54). As you pray about that, also include this: "Trustful dependence on Jesus makes victory not only possible but certain" (*In Heavenly Places,*17).

# 4

# Embrace Family Prayer

**"There he built an altar to the Lord and called on the name of the Lord" (Genesis 12:8).**

Can you identify the "he" in the above statement? The reference provides a good hint. Before reading further, reflect on these words: *He built an altar.* Do you see anything for this 21st century? Would you agree with the following paragraph?

As the family gathers for breakfast, the father, or the mother in the father's absence, should lead out in a short family worship. During these moments give thanks for the night's rest. Along with thanksgiving, let a petition for the protection of heavenly beings ascend heavenward—prayers so highly regarded by God that He compares them to incense, and puts Christ's righteousness with them (Revelation 8:3, 4).

Consider a comment about family prayer published in 1892:

> In many homes, prayer is neglected. Parents feel that they have no time for morning and evening worship. They cannot spare a few moments to be spent in thanksgiving to God for His abundant mercies,—for the blessed sunshine and the showers of rain, for the guardianship of holy angels. They have no time to offer prayer for divine help and guidance, and for the abiding presence of Jesus in the household (*Review and Herald,* 23 December 1902).

The same author used this illustration: "They go forth to labor as the horse or the ox goes, without one thought of God or heaven. . . . They have little more appreciation of his goodness than have the beasts that perish" (ibid.).

Recall the oxygen illustration in the previous chapter. Does that absence of prayer oxygen have a deadly effect?

Let's go to your home. Did your family consider a verse of Scripture, with a few moments of prayer, before you scattered this morning? Consider another suggestion:

> Parents, each morning consecrate yourselves and your family to God for that day. . . . One brief day is given you. As if it were your last on earth, work during its hours for the Master. . . . Eternity alone will reveal the good results with which such seasons of worship are fraught (*My Life Today,* 35).

For a word of encouragement:

> By sincere, earnest prayer parents should make a hedge about their children. They should pray with full faith that God will abide with them and that holy angels will guard them and their children from Satan's cruel power (*Testimonies for the Church,* 7:42, 43).

A small Andrews University religion class gave the following as some reasons for leaving out family worship:

- The family does not get up at the same time.
- People never have breakfast together, and leave at varied times.
- Some may be new members who have not yet been told about family worship.
- Others consider themselves too busy to take time for family prayer.

One soon-to-be-married young woman wrote, in effect: "In our family we never had morning worship. When I was little we almost always had evening worship. But no more."

**Habits! Habits! Habits!**

Some years ago, before I retired from pastoring, I gave a devotional talk about devotional habits. Texts included Matthew 6:33, on seeking first the kingdom of God, and the words of Jesus in Luke 11 about asking for God's Spirit. With each habit I had a Bible reference, with which I also included a Spirit of Prophecy sentence or a paragraph. Here I list these eight habits, the Bible reference and a sentence of comment. Two kinds of habits got intermingled: private habits and family habits.

1. Think of Jesus and reach out to Him as soon as you awake (Psalm 57:8, 9). "The very first outbreathing of the soul in the morning should be for the presence of Jesus" (*My Life Today,* 15).

2. Kneel at your bedside as you arise (Psalm 5:3). "When you rise in the morning, kneel at your bedside, and ask God to give you strength to fulfill the duties of the day, and to meet its temptations. . . . Ask Him to help you speak words that will inspire those around you with hope and courage, and draw you nearer to the Saviour" (*Sons and Daughters of God,* 199).

3. Spend unhurried time with your Bible (Jeremiah 15:16). "The heart that receives the Word of God . . . is like the mountain stream fed by unfailing springs" (*Christ's Object Lessons,* 130).

4. Spend a few moments in silent adoration of Jesus or the Father (John 14:1-3, 14). "Silently we may adore; for silence in this matter is the only eloquence. This love is past all language to describe" (*Fundamentals of Education,* 180).

5. Learn to pray without ceasing (1 Thessalonians 5:17). "The Christian whose heart is thus stayed upon God cannot be overcome" (*Messages to Young People,* 249).

6. Begin some kind of journaling plan, in which you record prayer requests, answers, providences, new ideas from your Bible study (1 Samuel 7:12). "Let such ones [those seeking to impart light] keep a diary, and when the Lord gives them an interesting experience, let them write it down, as Samuel did when the armies of Israel won a victory over the Philistines" (*The SDA Bible Commentary,* Ellen White comments, 2:1012).

7. Confess your sins at the close of each day (1 John 1:9). "Go to your rest at night with every sin confessed" (*Testimonies,* 9:48).

8. Let your last thought of the day be of God and His goodness (Psalms 4:8; 104:34). "Your last thought at night, your first thought in the morning, should be of Him in whom is centered your hope of eternal life" (*Our High Calling,* 116).

Remember this: thoughts tend to become an action, an action repeated becomes a habit, habits make character, and character determines where you will spend eternity. I learned something about forming habits from an article by William James that appeared in *Reader's Digest* (August 1967 reprint, 81-84, from August '37). I used it for *always* wearing a seat belt.

- Start immediately.
- Start strong (make yourself accountable to someone).
- Make no exceptions.
- Every day perform one voluntary act of self-denial.

The latter could be skipping a dessert or a between-meal snack, don't express an irritation, don't watch a usual TV program, etc. This conditions you to become a self-denying temperament. On seat belts the "no-exceptions" helps one become consistent!

**With the swiftness of lightning**

I am writing this on the Wednesday evening after the year 2000 election. At prayer meeting a week ago, Dwight Nelson of Andrews University's PMC (Pioneer

Memorial Church) suggested that tonight we would especially pray for the new president. That we could not do, with the election unsettled at that time. But Pastor Dwight had us turn to Ezekiel 1:14, which states, "The living creatures ran back and forth, in appearance like a flash of lightning."

In the margin of his Bible, Pastor Dwight said, he had noted that the last chapter of volume 5 of *Testimonies for the Church* contains comments about Ezekiel 1. As an assertion about verse 14, Ellen White wrote: "The bright light going among the living creatures with the swiftness of lightning represents the speed with which this work will finally go forward to completion" (754).

Compare these two sentences:

- The final movements will be rapid ones.
- This work will be completed with the swiftness of lightning.

Do they describe imminent developments?

**Application**

- Select one of the eight habits listed, then use the four suggestions about habits to develop a new devotional one.
- "Pray often. Plead with God to give you a spirit of supplication" (*Testimonies,* 5:590).

# 5

# Regard Midweek a Hundred-Dollar Event

**"And they continued steadfastly in the apostles' doctrine and fellowship, in the breaking of bread, and in prayers" (Acts 2:42).**

Suppose your pastor just inherited a half million dollars. He has focused on the above words, and decides the 10 percent of his membership that attends his prayer meeting needs to change. He and his wife decide that for one month they will hand out a hundred dollar bill each prayer-meeting night to each person who attends. "Just show up, bring your Bible," the pastor announces, "and a hundred dollars is yours."

Would you be there?

Glance again at the opening verse. The "they" implies a sizeable group; certainly more than a half dozen or dozen people. And certainly more than 5 or 10 percent of the 3,000 members baptized on the Day of Pentecost.

While I worked on this chapter, an undergrad couple named Brad and Bessie came to the table at the Andrews cafeteria where I ate lunch. I found out neither attended the AU prayer meeting. "I have too many studies," Bessie said.

I shared the above illustration with them, and asked their opinion about the hundred-dollar bill handout by the pastor. "Should I have him handing out $1,000 bills each time instead of $100?" I asked.

"I think not," said Brad. "A hundred dollars every week for four weeks would be $400! That would get me to come."

"Wouldn't the added awareness of the presence of Christ," I asked, "do more for you than hundred dollar bills?"

They agreed it should. We then discussed two things that lessen the interest of youth: song services without enthusiasm and prayer groups where participants offer long prayers.

For the song service, they suggested using some hymns that appeal to older folk, such as "The Old Rugged Cross," and some like "Make Me a Sanctuary," that appeal more to young adults. "Intermingle the two kinds," they advised.

We then talked about boredom from lengthy prayers. I mentioned that prayer conferences often used what they call "popcorn praying." "No prayers longer than one sentence, and no going around the circle," I explained, "but people are encouraged to pray a sentence prayer two or more times. The spontaneity increases interest." Both Brad and Bessie liked that idea.

**Making a difference**

The cover for *Fresh Wind, Fresh Fire* (Zondervan, 1997) tells that when the youthful Jim Cymbala started pastoring the Brooklyn Tabernacle congregation in 1972, it drew barely twenty people to a Sunday service. The sanctuary consisted of a shabby two-story building that needed paint. Its location? A part of New York where prostitutes, pimps, drug addicts, and homeless people seemed to rule. Early in his ministry Cymbala told the people:

> I want to say to you today with all the seriousness I can muster: *From this day on, the prayer meeting will be the barometer of our church. What happens on Tuesday night will be the gauge by which we judge success or failure because that will be the measure by which God blesses us* (27).

God promises to bless, he told his people, if they call upon the Lord to: (1) bring the unsaved to Himself, and (2) pour out His Spirit. If they did not:

> God has promised nothing—nothing at all. It's as simple as that. No matter what I preach or what we claim to believe in our heads, the future will depend upon our times of prayer (ibid.).

It took time, but with his continued emphasis the Tuesday night prayer meeting did become well attended. And the church? The cover of the book reported: "Today it is six thousand strong, a testament of what God can do when men and women begin to pour out their hearts to God."

At Cymbala's church, of the Assembly of God faith, all who pray apparently do so simultaneously—a style most churches never use. *But those who attend do pray. And with compassion!* Whatever its style, fervent prayer blended with Bible compassion makes a difference!

Cymbala has prepared a noncopyright video that could be shown for midweek service. In it he focuses on the words of Jesus, " ' "My house shall be called a house of prayer" ' " (Matthew 21:13). In the video, as he speaks to a praise service at another location, he shares his experience at the New York Tabernacle, and tells of the conversion of a daughter whom he and his wife had lost to the world during their early years at the New York Tabernacle.

The video, and the book *Fresh Wind, Fresh Fire,* are available from Zondervan Publishers. If your church has a lending library, you could consider stocking it with a half dozen or more books and several videos.

**Why some don't attend**

Would the following be imaginary for *your* congregation? Your pastor makes an announcement similar to this, and follows it with a new emphasis on intercessory prayer.

> *From this day on, the prayer meeting will be the barometer of our church. What happens on that night will be the gauge by which we judge our success or failure.*

Now connect imagination with two texts:

- " 'I will pour on the house of David . . . the Spirit of grace and supplication' " (Zechariah 12:10).
- "I pour out my soul" (Psalm 42:4).

Note the contrast. God "pours out" a spirit of supplication. We "pour out" our souls. Could a "pouring out," if by thousands, usher in a new Pentecost? Could it bring "the second coming of the Holy Spirit"?

I once asked a small seminary class of six people what percent of their home church came out for prayer meeting. It averaged 10 to 15 percent, with one exception—at one time at Oakwood, 70 percent of the attending members and students also came to prayer meeting. I then asked the class why, in their opinion, nonattenders didn't come. Answers included:

- Some feel that prayer meeting has no bearing on their salvation.
- Others feel a midweek service tends to be a boring waste of time.
- The meetings lack forethought and power.
- People don't realize how much our church needs group prayer for the Holy Spirit.

Here are some words as to what prayer meeting should be like:

> The prayer meetings should be the most interesting gatherings that are held, but these are frequently poorly managed. Many attend preaching, but neglect the prayer meeting. Here, again, thought is required.

> Wisdom should be sought of God, and plans should be laid to conduct the meetings so that they will be interesting and attractive. The people hunger for the bread of life. If they find it at the prayer meeting they will go there to receive it (*Testimonies for the Church,* 4:70).

For more in ideas, get volume 4, and read the first seven pages of the chapter titled "Co-workers With Christ." Give much attention to pages 70 and 71. See also the 6-page chapter in volume 2 titled "Social Meetings."

Here's another suggestion:

> When in the house of God, we should pray for a present blessing and should expect God to hear and answer our prayers. Such meetings will be lively and interesting (*Testimonies,* 1:145).

**Application**

- Ask your church to order two or several copies of *Fresh Wind, Fresh Fire* and one of the videos that illustrate it. Then encourage as many as possible to read the book and watch the video.
- If you are a pastor or elder scheduled to speak, present the key ideas in this chapter to your congregation. If possible, show a small part of the video during the 11:00 service.
- If you are a pastor or leader, consider sharing the 6-page chapter of volume 2 titled "Social Meetings," or pages 70 and 71 of the volume 4 chapter titled "Co-workers With Christ." Distribute these as widely as possible to your members. You may want to explain that prayer meetings used to be called "social meetings."

# 6

# Cling to Christ's Worthiness

**"He made Him who knew no sin to be sin for us, that we might become the righteousness of God in Him" (2 Corinthians 5:21).**

When armies march no one has certainty that he'll survive. In World War II Roy Boehm was one on the destroyer *Duncan* when it was sunk near Guadalcanal on October 12, 1942, after being hit by fifty-two Japanese shells. He said: "The plunge overboard drove me into dark, warm waters. I fought to hold on to my senses. If I passed out I would just keep sinking. I was 18, and I had shrapnel in both legs and in my skull."

He held on to an injured shipmate, Dubiel, who was out of his mind with pain from severe burns. Wearing lifejackets, they had gone into the water about midnight. About daylight, they became aware they were not alone. "I saw fins cutting through the water like blades," he said. As one headed toward them, he added, "My foot was bleeding. The shark's fin disappeared beneath the surface. I spun in the water, my eyes searching frantically." Suddenly the friend he had been towing was jerked away, screaming, and then was gone. "I heard Dubiel's screams for years afterward," he said (*Newsweek,* 8 March1999, 49).

In the great controversy, Satan uses sharks too. "I'm going to hell anyway. So why try?" an eleventh-grade girl blurted out. I knew this young woman and mistakenly thought her to be strong spiritually. Like Roy with his friend, I will never forget her exclamation. It has motivated me to say more and still more about the security found through faith in Christ's mercies and merits.

**Trusting Jesus for security**

The simplicity of God's plan can be summed up with the single line cited at the start of this chapter. It describes it as a transaction: We give—surrender—the only thing we have, a sinful heart. In return Jesus gives us His righteousness.

For those of his day who trusted in their own goodness, Isaiah exclaimed, "All our righteousnesses are like filthy rags" (Isaiah 64:6). But once we make that "transaction," we love to pray, and to join others as they pray. Just as a fellow and girl who develop an attraction for each other find it natural to talk together, so the person who loves Christ loves to talk to Him both privately, and with others.

Many churches include a Garden of Prayer at the time of the pastoral prayer. It generally gets introduced like his: "If you have a need or problem that needs prayer, or if you have a special thanksgiving, please come to the front and join those from the platform who will be coming down to kneel with the one who offers the pastoral prayer."

Why do so few come? Why? Why? Why? Why a hesitation to pray aloud? Why a reluctance to even be seen on our knees when someone else prays?

What about the following as possible reasons?

- not feeling worthy; not good enough
- not seeing our Father as interested
- not thinking of Jesus as a Friend
- shyness, timidity
- a feeble understanding about prayer

You probably could suggest still others. But let's start with the final one. In the context about the need for prayer at home, in church, consider this observation: "The efficiency of earnest prayer is but feebly understood" (*Selected Messages,* 1:116).

*But feebly understood!* Hopefully, this book will bring some increased understandings as we look at other reasons, and as we see the tremendous difference that prayer can make.

**Not good enough**

At my Workshop in Prayer class, fall of 2000, we had only one chapter yet to read in Roger Morneau's *The Incredible Power of Prayer* (our text for the semester). The title of that chapter? "Feeling Unforgiven."

As we surveyed the study questions for that chapter, a fellow named Reggie raised his hand. "I think I see a major reason so many students and others don't pray: They don't feel forgiven; they don't feel good enough."

In that final chapter, "Feeling Unforgiven," Roger Morneau said he found this a far greater problem than he had realized. "It devastates me," he said, "when I read letters from lonely Christians who are convinced the shadows of their old sins are still following them. In other words, they feel God still holds their sins against them. After telling of the evil things they did before accepting Christ, many have asked, 'How could God forgive such wickedness?' " (119).

"Many of God's people have a hard time accepting the fact that God has really forgiven all their sins," he added (120). Part of this, Morneau thought, comes from not knowing Bible verses that deal with forgiveness.

We had just had our first snow, and before our start-of-class prayer, I cited a promise the students had underlined. " 'Though your sins are like scarlet, they shall be as white as snow' " (Isaiah 1:18). With that I reviewed other similar promises:

- **The Deep Sea Promise:** "He will again have compassion on us, and will subdue our iniquities. You will cast all our sins into the depths of the sea" (Micah 7:19).
- **The East-West Promise:** "As far as the east is from the west, so far has He removed our transgressions from us" (Psalm 103:12).
- **The Amnesia Promise:** " 'For I will forgive their iniquity, and their sin I will remember no more' " (Jeremiah 31:34).

**Not sensing Christ's desire for friendship**

In John 15, Jesus told the disciples, and us: " 'No longer do I call you servants, for a servant does not know what his master is doing; but I have called you friends, for all things that I heard from My Father I have made known to you' " (John 15:15). Jesus reflects the Father, and Both are glad to claim you as a friend. *Steps to Christ* offers an insight, a definition: "Prayer is the opening of the heart to God as to a friend" (93).

James urges, "The Lord is very compassionate and merciful (James 5:11). *Steps to Christ* cites the words of James, and comments: "His heart of love is touched by our sorrows and even by our utterances of them. Take to Him everything that perplexes the mind" (100). Ellen White then adds, "There is no perplexity too difficult for Him to unravel. No calamity can befall the least of His children, no anxiety harass the soul, no joy cheer, no sincere prayer escape the lips, . . . in which He takes no immediate interest" (ibid.).

What a Friend! And a Friend with unlimited power. Striking! He takes *an immediate interest* in our every anxiety, every joy, every sincere prayer.

**Timidity**

I know someone so timid that in grade school her timidity kept her from answering a question the teacher asked in a discussion even if she knew the answer. In every church there are some that shy. More than a hundred years ago the author of volume 4 of *Testimonies for the Church* wrote that long, prosy talks and prayers are out of place at prayer meeting or anywhere. She added:

> Those who are forward and ever ready to speak are allowed to crowd out the testimony of the timid and retiring. Those who are the

> most superficial generally have the most to say. Their prayers are long and mechanical. They weary the angels and the people who listen to them. Our prayers should be short and right to the point. Let the long, tiresome petitions be left for the closet, if any have such to offer (70, 71).

The solution? Consider one option: Prayer conferences often pray and study in groups of eight or ten. Each group meets four or five times during a weekend, with the same student leading out. Leaders come early, and are trained how to lead. Each gets trained to notice which of their group has very little to say. The leader would then call on them by name, with questions such as:

- Patty, would you read verse 10, and tell what you see in it?
- Patty, what do you think?
- Patty, could this situation have been handled another way?

**A parable uses an undergarment**

The Hebrew people did not generally cleave to God. As Jeremiah brings out again and again, they refused to listen. During Jeremiah's time our God, now almost desperate, tried one final time to get this point across. Think about an illustration I sometimes use in class: I put a pair of men's shorts in a paper sack, and offer extra points to any telling what's in the sack. I give three hints:

- The Bible has half a chapter about this garment.
- This garment was worn in Bible times.
- This garment still gets worn today.

I get all kinds of guesses: sandals, robes, hats, etc. But almost never the right one, until I share something from my now-out-of-print first book about prayer, *Whatever It Takes Praying*. Through the prophet Jeremiah God used a loin cloth, or as the TEV words it, a pair of men's shorts, as an object lesson:

> The Lord told me to go and buy myself some linen shorts and to put them on; but he told me not to put them in water. So I bought them and put them on. Then the Lord spoke to me again and said, "Go to the Euphrates River and hide the shorts in a hole in the rocks." So I went and hid them near the Euphrates (Jeremiah 13:1-5, TEV).

Some time later the Lord told Jeremiah to go back to the Euphrates and get the shorts. He did, but found them rotten. God then told Jeremiah that the rotten shorts represented His people. In their stubborn rejection of Him, and in their worship of other gods, they had ruined themselves.

**Two powerful truths**

May I suggest two important truths?

1. God wants His people to cling to Him the way an undergarment clings to the body.

2. If we don't cling to God, sin will erode our faith and make us like a rotten pair of shorts.

Think how different the history of this planet would have been if the Hebrew people had clung to God the way an undergarment clings to the body! How does one cling to God? Let me suggest:

• Embrace Jesus as your personal Savior at the beginning of each new day.

The word "embrace" means to clasp in the arms, readily and gladly. It means to hug, to cherish, to eagerly receive.

• Develop a strong faith in God's Word and in its promises.

We especially need to cleave to this fact: Christ shed blood. Mention that blood when tempted, whether by evil angels or their chief. Give thanks for this: "You cannot save yourself from the tempter's power, but he trembles and flees when the merits of that precious blood are urged" (*Testimonies*, 5:317).

**Application**

- For a concise summary read the chapter in *Steps to Christ* titled "Confession."
- In 1988 Pacific Press published a book by Thurman C. Petty, Jr. titled *Fire in the Gates* that may be in your church library. Chapter 9, "The Linen Belt," tells about Jeremiah's two trips. If you can borrow it to read for worship, your teens in particular will find it fascinating.
- The above book has Jeremiah's secretary Baruch going with him. From Jerusalem to the Euphrates? Some 350 miles each way, taking about three weeks one way. Two round trips total 1,400 miles of walking to make a point. What do you see as that point? Or points?

# 7

# Call for Angels to Help

**"The angel did wondrously, and Manoah and his wife looked on" (Judges 13:19, American Translation).**

I included the above for parents of little ones and for parents-to-be. You can find the full story of two parents and their concern for a child yet unborn in Judges 13. An angel had told Manoah's wife that she would have a son and that the child should never have strong drink or eat unclean meat. Then the father-to-be prayed, " 'O Lord, please let the man from God come back to us again and give us more instructions about the child you are going to give us.' The Lord answered his prayer, and the Angel of God appeared once again to his wife as she was sitting in the field. . . .

"She quickly ran and found her husband and told him, 'The same man is here again!'

"Manoah ran back with his wife and asked, 'Are you the man who talked to my wife the other day?'

" 'Yes,' he replied, 'I am.'

"So Manoah asked him, 'Can you give us any special instructions about how we should raise the baby after he is born?'

"And the Angel replied, 'Be sure that your wife follows the instructions I gave her' " (Judges 13:8-14, TLB).

Those instructions had to do with food! From this story *The Ministry of Healing* draws lessons about pre-natal influence. "In the words spoken to the Hebrew mother, God speaks to all mothers in every age. . . . The well-being of the child will be affected by the habits of the mother. Her appetites and passions are to be controlled by principle" (372).

*Her* appetites! What the mother-to-be eats really matters too! For more details see page 373 in *The Ministry of Healing.* The author gets very specific: "If before the birth of her child she is self-indulgent, if she is selfish, impatient, and exacting, these traits will be reflected in the disposition of the child. . . . But if the mother unswervingly adheres to right principles, if she is temperate and self-denying, if she is kind, gentle, and unselfish, she may give her child these same precious traits of character" (ibid., 372, 373).

**Angels and little ones**

Jesus took a special interest in children. Matthew 18 and 19 record three examples of His love for and deep interest in little ones, with commentary in a *Desire of Ages* chapter titled "Blessing the Children." The latter explains that "wherever the Saviour went, the benignity of His countenance, and His gentle, kindly manner won the love and confidence of children" (511). "He, the Majesty of heaven, did not disdain to answer their questions, and simplify His important lessons to meet their childish understanding" (ibid., 515).

Every parent would do well to read Matthew 19:13-15 and the above chapter again and again. And don't miss the parable of the one lost sheep in Matthew 18:12-14—a parable Jesus had told earlier in Luke 15, and which in Matthew 18 He adapted because of His love and concern for children.

Parents, this is for you: "Earnest, heartfelt prayers are to bring the angels near" (*Welfare Ministry,* 32). "We may in earnest, contrite prayer call the heavenly helpers to our side" (*Selected Messages,* 1:97). "Invisible armies of light and power attend the meek and lowly ones who believe and claim the promises of God" (*Christ's Object Lessons,* 176).

Space doesn't permit a full summary here about the work of angels, but consider: "We need to understand better than we do the mission of the angel visitants. It would be well to consider that in all our work we have the co-operation and care of heavenly beings" (ibid.).

*It would be well to consider!* Two more statements:

> When the earthborn children know it not, they have the angels of light as their companions (*Our High Calling,* 23).

> I have been shown angels of God all ready to impart grace and power to those who feel their need of divine strength. But these heavenly messengers will not bestow blessings unless solicited. . . . Often they have waited in vain (ibid., 129).

This, too, I see as a truth to never forget:

> Angels of heaven are passing throughout the length and breadth

> of the earth, seeking to comfort the sorrowing, to protect the imperiled, to win the hearts of men to Christ. Not one is neglected or passed by. God . . . has an equal care for all (*The Desire of Ages,* 639).

**More about the blood of Jesus**

Angels do a lot more than most people realize. But that's not all. Chapter 6 mentioned the blood of Jesus. " ' "It is the blood that makes atonement for the soul" ' " (Leviticus 17:11). In the margin of that text in my Bible I wrote this:

> The blood of Jesus is pleading with power and efficacy for those who are backslidden, for those who are rebellious, for those who sin against great light and love. . . . He is making intercession for the most lowly, the most oppressed and suffering, for the most tried and tempted ones (*Our High Calling,* 49).

Six groups Christ's blood pleads for at this very moment:

- the backslidden
- the rebellious
- those ignoring light
- the most lowly
- the most suffering
- the most tempted

**An invitation**

"Call on the Father . . . knowing that you were not redeemed with corruptible things, like silver or gold, from your aimless conduct . . . but with the precious blood of Christ" (1 Peter 1:17-19). The context tells one of the fabulous results: "So that your faith and hope are in God" (1:21). This again, from the last chapter: The tempter "trembles and flees when the merits of that precious blood are urged" (*Testimonies for the Church,* 5:317). May I suggest special attention to the word "urge"? When added to our prayers it offers much, especially as we pray for the latter rain. From the 2000 book *Great Prayers and Pray-ers of the Bible* I am borrowing these words about "urge":

Urge is from the Latin *urgere,* to press hard. Meanings include to prod, to push, to entreat, to implore, to beseech. Beseech meanings include "to ask for earnestly, solicit eagerly." Let's unite at the foot of the cross to really *press hard.*

As you pray, take the following as God's message to you: " 'I promise that I'll bless you with everything I have—bless and bless and bless!' " (Hebrews 6:14, *The Message*).

**Application**

- What idea in this chapter do you most need at the present time? Write it on a 3-by-5 card, keep it with you, and make it frequent subject matter for prayer.
- A truth to use as you intercede: "A silent witness guards every soul that lives, seeking to win and draw him to Christ. As long as there is hope, until they resist the Holy Spirit to their eternal ruin, men are guarded by heavenly intelligences."

# 8

# Watch Jesus in Prayer

**" 'Sanctify them by Your truth. Your word is truth' " (John 17:17).**

Wouldn't you enjoy listening to a cassette tape that contained one of the prayers of Jesus?

The Gospels refer fifteen times to the prayer life of Jesus, though only John 17 gives the wording of an actual prayer. I think I would choose that John 17 prayer, from which the above comes.

In imagination join me as we look in on the second giving of the Lord's Prayer, recorded in Luke 11. Let's ask, What to see? What to hear? What to feel?

Watch as one morning Jesus rises early and goes apart to pray. In your imagination, try to see two things:

- Jesus kneels at the base of a tree not far from Capernaum. Sunlight streams through the branches. For a moment you gaze on Christ's upturned face. You sense that as He talks to His Father—your God and His God—He seems to be in the very presence of God Himself. He prays aloud. His tone is quiet, yet earnest and confident.
- Watch as twelve men walk up. They say nothing, but listen as Jesus prays. Finally He says a quiet "Amen!" One of the disciples exclaims, "Lord, teach us to pray."

The next twelve verses (Luke 11:2-13) tell what Jesus told them about prayer on that occasion. We noted in chapter 6 that "the efficiency of earnest prayer [was and is] but feebly understood" (*Selected Messages,* 1:116). A careful study of Luke 11:1-13 can help a great deal. The following commentaries also offer ideas:

- the chapter in *Thoughts From the Mount of Blessing* titled "The Lord's Prayer"
- the chapter in *Christ's Object Lessons* titled "Asking to Give"

As I read devotional books compiled from the writings of Ellen White—like *My Life Today, In Heavenly Places,* etc.—I sometimes find a comment or insight to a Bible truth, which makes such an impact on me that I think I would not trade it for a thousand dollar bill. That happened on a recent weekend, as I went through the January readings for the 1964 book *That I May Know Him.*

I had read that book some years ago, underlined striking thoughts, then wrote key phrases (with page numbers) on the inside front and back covers. As I reviewed what I had underlined, the following comment—an insight about the prayer life of Jesus—seemed so revolutionary that I thought to myself: "That truth could help me pray more effectively than ever before!" Here's the sentence:

> His constant prayer for them (His disciples) was that they might be sanctified through the truth, and He prayed with assurance, knowing that an almighty decree had been given before the world was made (37).

The context adds "that truth, armed with the omnipotence of the Holy Spirit, would conquer in the contest with evil" (ibid.).

From John 17:17 and the preceding insights, four truths stand out:

- The truths of God's Word sanctify.
- Jesus "prayed constantly" that His people might experience that sanctifying influence.
- He prayed "with assurance."
- He knew "that truth, armed with the omnipotence of the Holy Spirit, would conquer in the contest with evil."

**We can pray the same way**

Do you see why I regard that new insight on John 17:17 as worth more than a thousand dollar bill? Consider these reasons:

- Truths that sanctify—that really change people—give us reason to praise God continually.
- I have been praying, as I brought out repeatedly in an earlier book, that God will raise up one million Spirit-filled followers. I can now urge that request with a new assurance.
- The Holy Spirit possesses omnipotence—and that omnipotence guarantees that truth contains an omnipotent power.

Chapter 2 of the book *More and Still More,* has this title: "100,000 Spirit-filled

Youth." The same chapter urged readers to pray that God will also raise up another 100,000 Spirit-filled older folk: lay persons, pastors, leaders.

Then as I prepared the book *Great Prayers and Pray-ers of the Bible,* world membership of the Adventist Church passed 11,000,000. I suggest that we should pray that God will raise up *at least one million* fully surrendered and Spirit-filled people: a quarter million such young women, a quarter million such young men, and a half million older folk. I pray God will use them to motivate millions of the other eleven million to make a full, prayer-filled surrender.

I can now pray that with new assurance. So can you. The truths of God's Word sanctify. They truly do, as an illustration in the next section of this chapter illustrates.

The word *omnipotent* means "all powerful." Synonymous words or phrases include almighty, supreme, unlimited power, unlimited authority. These words describe what the Holy Spirit possesses! And we work with Him as our Partner!

**Truth's transforming power**

John Quade, one of the fastest milers in the United States with a time of 3:54.6, moved to Sacramento to train for the 1992 Olympics. Hampered by an injury, and unable to compete in the Olympics, he still managed to earn money by running races all over the world as a paid athlete. "But even though I was winning races and had all the free Nike shoes and products one could want, I felt restless and unsatisfied," he said. "I knew something crucial was missing in my life."

In 1992 he quit professional running and shifted his emphasis to making money. He thought that money would give him the peace he longed to find. He had done much of his running in the hills of California, and hoped to earn enough to buy some property in the mountains. While working in the mortgage banking industry, he read a biography of Bill Gates. Inspired, he started a software business and experienced considerable success. Earning money became exciting and addicting.

Something still seemed missing. He asked his mom to get him a Bible for Christmas. He started reading it even though he understood little. "For the first time in many years," he said, "I decided to attend church one Sunday. I went Bible in hand, eager to learn all I could. I was deeply disappointed when they didn't even open the Scriptures once during the service and no one spoke to me or shook my hand." After the service he sat in his car and wept.

He decided to continue to save as much money as possible, and accepted a full-time position in a Money Store in its information technology division. About that time John received a handbill for a prophecy seminar at the Sacramento Central Church. He had studied American economics, and the topic, "The USA in Prophecy," intrigued him. "Does the Bible talk about the USA?" he asked himself. "I've got to hear this!"

The opening night he met a businessman named Steve who sat with him in the back row. "I'm a Presbyterian," Steve told John, and asked, "What denomination are you?"

John responded, "I'm a Lutheran." As the speaker explained the Scriptures, both men would look at each other with their mouths gaping. "Have you ever heard anything like this before?" they would ask. By the second night, as the Amazing Facts evangelist Kim Jajer showed how the Bible had predicted historical events, both men were hooked.

"How come no one ever told us the Bible prophecies were true?" they said. They came back night after night, and often stood in the parking lot, excitedly discussing what they had just learned (Amazing Facts Newsletter, November 2000).

**Application**

- Copy John 17:17 and how Jesus felt about it (page 39) onto a 3-by-5 card, keep it with you, and use it to pray with more and still more assurance.
- Pencil in hand, read the chapter in *Christ's Object Lessons* titled "Asking to Give." Put a check by each new insight about Luke 11:1-13.

# 9

# Praise God for His Mercy

**"Oh, give thanks to the Lord, for He is good! For His mercy endures forever" (Psalm 136:1).**

Psalm 136 repeats "For His mercy endures forever" at the end of each verse. For temple worship, either the worshipers or a choir sang this psalm as a response. Perhaps you have noticed that one finds much song in Bible religion. Someone has said:

> Atheism is songless; agnosticism has nothing to sing about; the various forms of idolatry are not tuneful; but Judaism said, "O Come, let us sing to the Lord," and when Christ came, the angels greeted His birth with praise.*

Psalm 136 attaches God's mercy to many "great wonders" (v. 4)—the heavens, the layout of the earth, the sun to rule by day, the moon and stars to rule by night, Israel's departure from Egypt, the overthrow of Pharaoh and his army, the rescue of Israel from other enemies, leading them through the wilderness, manna, etc.

Put yourself with the Hebrews as the following took place:

> To Him who divided the Red Sea in two,
> For His mercy endures forever;
> And made Israel pass through the midst of it,
> For His mercy endures forever;
> But overthrew Pharaoh and his army in the Red Sea,
> For His mercy endures forever (Psalm 136:13-15).

Turn time back to when Moses lived, and imagine yourself as one of the two million people who left Egypt, only to get to the Red Sea to end up trapped there—mountains on both sides, the Egyptians behind, and the sea ahead. Then you watch Moses lift his rod, and the waters divide. You and your family were the first to enter the sea. With amazement you glance up toward the walls of water on both sides, but the road is dry, and all press ahead. In due time, you reach the farther shore, and gratefully step onto the desert sand. Finally the last family, the last lamb, the last wagon reaches the shore. Arthur Maxwell gives this description of how everyone must have felt:

> A sigh of relief goes up from everybody as, looking back, they see the channel is clear! Everybody has got across! No one is left behind!
>
> But look! What is that moving on the shore they have just left? Spears! Swords! Chariots! The Egyptians! See! They are rushing down the opposite bank! They are coming right through the channel between the walls of water!
>
> "O God!" cry the people in their fear and anguish. "O God, help us! Save us from the Egyptians!" (*The Bible Story*, 2: 134).

And God does save you. The walls of water collapse and the Egyptians disappear beneath the waves.

Have you been able to put yourself into the picture? Perhaps as a young husband with a wife and little boy? Or as a teenage girl? Or as a grandmother? Or as a fellow whose life was saved by the blood on the doorpost?

What would that nighttime crossing have been like for you? As the Egyptians lash out at their chariot horses, can you picture them? Can you see Moses holding out his rod? Can you hear the shriek of the wind? Can you see the foam-capped billows?

**Come, let us sing to the Lord**

For the next few paragraphs, picture yourself as still on the shores of the Red Sea, surrounded by a vast defenseless crowd of two million people—slaves unused to battle, fathers, husbands, young men, women, children. All are now free! What emotions would be surging through your heart, and theirs?

Their enemies are no more! All the credit goes to God. The Spirit of God rests upon Moses, and he leads the vast multitude in an anthem of praise: the earliest and one of the most sublime known to man. Moses begins, and the men join in. Then Miriam leads the way as the song is taken up by the women. "Far over desert and sea rang the joyous refrain, and the mountains re-echoed the words of their praise" (*Patriarchs and Prophets*, 289).

If you have the above book, and want this chapter to become still more real, read the commentary on Exodus 14 and 15 (chapter 25). This song, and the deliverance it commemorates, made an impression never to be forgotten by the Hebrew people. And as the above book points out, that song belongs to this generation also:

> That song does not belong to the Jewish people alone. It points forward to the destruction of all the foes of righteousness and the final victory of the Israel of God (289).

As we approach a similar deliverance, song can be a part of every prayer meeting. Note the following suggestion:

> Music can be a great power for good, yet we do not make the most of this branch of worship. . . . Music should have beauty, pathos, and power. Let the voices be lifted in songs of praise and devotion. Call to your aid, if practicable, instrumental music, and let the glorious harmony ascend to God (*Testimonies for the Church,* 4:71).

The context offers still other suggestions: about guidance of strong-minded singers, about common sense, about the need for the Spirit of God in the heart. The strong focus on the need for "sympathy and sociability with one another" (ibid.) at worship services such as prayer meeting implies that testimonies could be intermingled with the music.

As mentioned elsewhere, no prosy prayers or testimonies. Too often those who are forward and ever ready to speak are allowed to crowd out those who are timid and retiring (ibid., 70). To help correct this situation, one could photocopy the above two pages for distribution to the entire congregation. This advice to a Brother N. about his testimony, published in 1876, could be shared:

> A few pointed words in relation to your progress in the divine life, spoken in a clear, audible voice, in an earnest manner . . . would be edifying to others and a blessing to your own soul (*Testimonies,* 4:132).

As a guide for all who give a testimony at prayer meeting, we do well to underline *a few pointed words.* Also: *clear, audible voice.*

**Application**

- For family worship, or for prayer meeting, use Exodus 15 and some of the ideas here. Consider also the vivid words in volume 4 of the *Testimonies* chapter titled "Go Forward."

# 10

# Welcome Farmer God's Pruning

**" 'I am the vine, you are the branches. He who abides in Me, and I in him, bears much fruit; for without Me you can do nothing' " (John 15:5).**

Ever think of God as a Farmer? Here is an interesting wording of the above:

> "I am the Real Vine and my Father is the Farmer. He cuts off every branch of me that doesn't bear grapes. And every branch that is grape-bearing he prunes back so it will bear even more" (John 15:1, *The Message*).

The end verses of the John 15:1-8 passage promises: " 'If you abide in Me, and My words abide in you, you will ask what you desire, and it shall be done . . . By this My Father is glorified, that you bear much fruit' " (John 15:7, 8).

Let's say you love gardening. You set out a few tomato plants and plant a couple of hills of cucumbers. A few crocuses, daffodils, and tulips delight you with their spring blooms. In your yard you planted a redbud, a couple of Rose of Sharon trees, a clematis vine, a Concord grape, two fruit trees, and some roses.

Each is special to you as you watch its progress. Each gets loving care. All except the bulbs need pruning. Every cut is made with care. You want every tree to make maximum growth, with a good shape and lots of buds and blooms. The grapevine, like the vine in the above text, gets pruned so that it will "bear even more" than it otherwise would.

The paraphrase cited above has Jesus saying: "My Father is the Farmer." I see each person who seeks to be Spirit-filled and fruitful as one of God's favorite plants. Each has special qualities, which adds new beauty.

**No one like you**

My wife has four house cats—Sparkle, Buttons, Buddy, and Tiger. Tiger is my favorite. I almost always include corn flakes in my breakfast, and Tiger always comes around to beg for a few. He showed up in our back yard as a small kitten, apparently cast off, and it took my wife a week to get him to come out of the garden plants to the patio for cat food. She named him Tiger because of his stripes, and little by little she enticed him into the house, and got him to use a litter pan. An eight-year-old granddaughter who tried to make friends with him exclaimed, "Tiger, you are so cute I can't stand it." He sometimes will let her pet him, but all four cats possess a distrust of strangers, and generally disappear if they hear a car in the driveway.

Each cat is precious, but quite different from each other—just as humans are. God apparently intended it that way, and longs to save every one. So does Jesus, as the parable of the one lost sheep shows. To Him, one percent of the one hundred sheep of Luke 15 mattered. It is the same with people. He would have died for just one.

**No needless pruning**

In a sense shy, frightened little Tiger got a lot of pruning. Through her gentle methods my wife pruned away his fright, his distrust of humans, and his shyness.

Does Jesus deal as kindly with us as He prunes away pride, lust, selfishness, or whatever? Notice this statement:

> For we do not have a High Priest who cannot sympathize with our weaknesses. . . . Let us therefore come boldly to the throne of grace, that we may obtain mercy and find grace to help in time of need (Hebrews 4:15, 16).

"Mercy" and "help in time of need." Think for a moment what *time of need* could include. Which of the following would be the hardest for you to bear?

- a terminal illness
- an auto accident in which a family member does not survive
- an upcoming surgery for which the outcome is in doubt
- a tornado destroys your home
- a huge medical bill for which you have no insurance
- loss of a driver's license

Would the above passage from Hebrews remind you that you have resources not available to non-Christians? David summed up those advantages by pointing out, "Many sorrows shall be to the wicked; but he who trusts in the Lord, mercy shall surround him" (Psalm 32:10).

We could ask, "What are the mercies of which David speaks? What advantages does the religion of Christ offer?" Let's start with a few of the mercies.

## Help when things go wrong

Are the wicked free from disappointment, perplexity, earthly losses, poverty, and distress? The devotional book *Our High Calling* notes that when sickness and death come, they lean on their own resources—with no strengthening grace from a Higher Power. As death approaches, "they obtain no consolation by looking forward to the future, but a fearful uncertainty torments them; and thus they close their eyes in death, not finding any pleasure in looking forward to the resurrection morn, for they have no cheering hope that they shall have part in the first resurrection" (9).

The idea of being pruned may not appeal to you—cutting sounds horrible. But it makes you a far more wonderful person. And mercy, which we looked at in the previous chapter, actually enhances the pruning. By the time we get to the final chapter of this book—"More and More Like Jesus"—perhaps you will truly want more and more. Consider this prayer as not only the longing of Paul, but also the sentiments of Jesus Himself:

> This I pray, that your love may abound still more and more in knowledge and all discernment, that you may approve the things that are excellent, that you may be sincere and without offense till the day of Christ, being filled with the fruits of righteousness which are by Jesus Christ, to the glory and praise of God (Philippians 1:9-11).

What Christ wants pruning to accomplish is:

- For you to experience the above "being filled" with the "fruits of righteousness"—i.e., an ongoing, daily, becoming more and more like Him.
- For you to glorify your Father by bearing "much fruit" (John 15:8).

Here's a promise about that fruit bearing: "Those who sow in tears shall reap in joy. He who continually goes forth weeping, bearing seed for sowing, shall doubtless come again with rejoicing, bringing his sheaves with him" (Psalm 126:5, 6). The above prayer, if you pray it in behalf of others, will help make you ever more fruitful. Note the change of pronouns in the following "version":

> This I pray, that [their] love may abound still more and more in knowledge and all discernment, that [they] may approve the things that are excellent, that [they] may be sincere and without offense till the day of Christ, being filled with the fruits of righteousness which are by Jesus Christ, to the glory and praise of God" (Philippians 1:9-11).

## Application

- To become more fruitful, memorize and use the preceding prayer in behalf of anyone for whom you have a burden to see them become more like Jesus.

# 11

## Begin a Prayer Ministry

**"Rejoice always, pray without ceasing, in everything give thanks; for this is the will of God in Christ Jesus for you" (1 Thessalonians 5:16-18).**

As mentioned, for a text in Workshop in Prayer, we use Roger Morneau's *The Incredible Power of Prayer.* He begins the next-to-final chapter with these words; "Perhaps the question people most ask me is, 'How can a person begin a successful prayer ministry and keep it going? One that will enable me to actually see my prayers answered?' " (114).

He replies, "I have discovered five steps to follow that have demonstrated that they will bring the power of God into the lives of those you pray for" (ibid.).

In abbreviated form, the steps are:

**Step 1:** The key to any prayer ministry begins with a closer walk with Jesus. He is the chief soul winner, and longs to help each one of us share in His mission. That walk begins, he wrote, as soon as one opens his or her eyes in the morning. He gives a sample prayer of his own. On this I refer you back to chapter 3 of this book, "Start Everything With Prayer."

**Step 2:** A solid foundation is a must. Just as a house needs a solid foundation, so do those who seek to win others to Jesus. This begins, he says, with memorization of Scripture. In his pocket he carries pieces of paper upon which he has written verses of Scripture. He uses leisure moments to memorize, and in his forty-six years of ministry has memorized 2,200 verses.

With my students I follow a similar plan, though it consists of underlining eighty of the better known Old Testament promises, and eighty from the New Testament. Chapter 13 of this book deals with this. The course outline for my class includes six Bible prayers I ask students to underline. You will find samples at the close of this chapter.

**Step 3:** Compassionate love. This, he wrote, motivated Jesus to come to this planet and let wicked men nail Him to a cross. For a better understanding of how much that cost, read again Matthew 27, and underline each mention of blood, and each happening, such as the scourging, which brought blood. Get a copy of the Pacific Press book *The Gift.* Kim Johnson writes vividly about Christ's sufferings.

**Step 4:** A living faith. To develop faith, Morneau recommends much time reading the four Gospels—Matthew, Mark, Luke, and John. "Educate yourself," Ellen White suggested, "to have unlimited confidence in God" (*In Heavenly Places,* 71).

**A step you need every day!**

**Step 5:** Forgiveness. Morneau writes, "We live in an age when people do not find their prayers answered because they do not first ask God to forgive their own sins" (117). For this I recommend the verses about forgiveness found in the Lord's Prayer in Matthew 6:14, 15. See also the chapter in this book titled "Cling to Christ's Worthiness." If you have Morneau's *The Incredible Power of Prayer,* see the chapter titled "Feeling Forgiven."

For insights about feeling I go to the chapter "Faith and Acceptance" in *Steps to Christ.* It's fabulous! Consider this:

> You cannot change your heart and make yourself holy. But God promises to do all this for you through Christ. You *believe* that promise. You confess your sins and give yourself to God. You *will* to serve Him. Just as surely as you do this, God will fulfill His word to you. If you believe the promise,—believe that you are forgiven and cleansed,—God supplies the fact; you are made whole. . . . It *is* so if you believe it (51).

The author then appeals: "Do not wait to *feel* that you are made whole, but say, 'I believe it; it *is* so, not because I feel it, but because God has promised' " (ibid.).

**Specific Bible Prayers to Memorize**

Our publishing houses are promised that if there is prayer as work begins each day (and there is), angels would keep the machinery running efficiently. If angels perform that kind of ministry for machinery, how much more they minister when we pray for people! Keep in mind that this denomination, counting academies at self-supporting schools like Weimar and the Black Hills, operates nearly 1,000 secondary schools, along with almost 90 colleges and universities, and over 4,500 elementary schools. Total enrollment? Nearly one million! The first prayers I ask students to memorize deal especially with the potential for youth, as given here:

> Let Your work appear to Your servants, and Your glory [character: John 1:14] to their children. And let the beauty of the Lord our God be upon us, and establish the work of our hands for us; yes, establish the work of our hands (Psalm 90:16, 17).

Notice this phrase: *Let the beauty of the Lord our God be upon us.* I used that in two previous books: *30 Days to a More Powerful Prayer Life* and *Great Prayers and Pray-ers of the Bible.* I want to again urge you to memorize at least that phrase, and as you seek to pray without ceasing, use it again and again.

**All, all, all, always**

Space permits only one more suggestion, and for it I want to mention Psalm 67. It's another memory assignment—something else I want students to use for the Advent movement every day. The gospel commission, in Matthew 28:18-20, has "all" four times: *all* authority given, teach *all* nations, observe *all* things, I am with you *always.* Psalm 67 has *all* four times, too. It begins with this: "God be merciful to us and bless us, and cause His face to shine upon us. That Your way may be known on earth, Your salvation among *all* nations" (vs. 1, 2). Note the praise in the next verses:

> Let the peoples praise You, O God; let *all* the peoples praise You. Oh, let the nations be glad and sing for joy! For You shall judge the people righteously, and govern the nations on earth. Let the peoples praise You, O God; let *all* the peoples praise You (vs. 3-5).

I suggest that Psalm 67 is the Old Testament parallel to the Revelation 14:6 assurance that "every nation, tribe, tongue, and people" will be reached with the gospel. Psalm 67 ends this way: "Then the earth shall yield her increase; God, our own God, shall bless us. God shall bless us, and *all* the ends of the earth shall fear Him" (vs. 6, 7).

As you use Psalm 67 in your prayer ministry, note that it includes the word *all* four times—a use that parallels the commission of Christ in Matthew 28:18-20. When you pray that prayer, it can take place in North Korea, Saudi Arabia, Iran, Iraq, and all such mostly closed lands.

**Short but powerful prayers**

The entire book of Nehemiah shows the importance of prayer: His chapter 1 private prayer, His short but history-changing prayer in chapter 2, and prayers all through the book. But think about his prayer in chapter 2. With King Artaxerxes looking right at him, Nehemiah said later, "I prayed to the God of heaven" (2:4). He didn't kneel, or close his eyes, but that few-seconds, silent prayer reached the throne of the universe.

Here are a few short prayers I can send heavenward as I come and go:

- "Because of Christ's blood, all, all, all."

This prayer depends on this fact: Christ's blood, mentioned in prayer, causes Satan to tremble and flee.

- "Forgiven, clothed, transformed, filled."

As I pray for another, "forgiven" provides for his or her need for forgiveness. "Clothed" asks God to clothe that person with the righteousness of Jesus. "Transformed" requests that the person listen to and experience changes through God's Word. And "filled" asks that the person welcome and live a Spirit-filled life.

- "Make me [or a person you meet] a sanctuary."

"Make Me a Sanctuary" has become a favorite song with youth, and makes a meaningful prayer song even for retirees. Try praying the words, silently, for yourself, or for a person you meet, wording it "Make him (her) a sanctuary for You."

- "Whatever it takes."

Auto agencies often advertise they will do whatever it takes to get you into one of their new cars. Jesus was willing to do whatever it took to make salvation available to you, even though it cost Him unbelievable pain, even to death forsaken by God. And Paul, as 2 Corinthians 11:24-28 relates, had this whatever it takes list: five whippings, two beatings with rods, three shipwrecks, long journeys, hunger, thirst, cold without adequate clothing. When you pray for another, "whatever it takes," you invite God to really go into action for the person of your concern.

- Frequent "Thank You" to the Lord—whenever you see a changed life, flowers in bloom, a blue sky, rainfall, etc.

In 1885, in a letter to a family who had lost a daughter, and grieved unreasonably, Ellen White wrote a letter found in volume 5 of *Testimonies for the Church,* titled "Sinfulness of Repining." We too would do well to read it, for it described some of the wonders of nature. It includes these two sentences:

> I call your attention to these blessings from the bounteous hand of God. Let the fresh glories of each new morning awaken praise in your hearts for these tokens of His loving care (312).

Consider this suggestion: let continuous praise help you as you seek to "pray without ceasing." It will surround you with an atmosphere of prayer, which will make it natural to lift you thoughts in a prayer to God as you meet people needing your intercession, even when you breathe only a few words of silent petition such as listed above. You will think of other prayers as you develop a ministry of prayer.

**Application**

- Other Bible prayers to underline, and maybe to memorize and use: Ephesians 3:14-19; 1 Chronicles 29:10b-13; 2 Chronicles 20:6, 12; Nehemiah 9:5b, 6; Psalm 5:1-3, 11, 12; Psalm 9:1, 2; Daniel 9:8, 9, Colossians 1:9-14
- Revelation 14:6 mandates that the three angels' messages will go "to every nation"—including Moslem lands. Join us in a goal to use Psalm 67 many times a day in behalf of the entire world field.
- The more than 40,000 congregations of the world church form 12 divisions, with a total of 92 unions. The 92 unions have a total of 447 conferences and missions. Pray daily for an entire division. God "is able" (Ephesians 3:20).

# 12

# Seek Spirit-Filled Living

**" 'I will pray the Father, and He will give you another Helper, that He may abide with you forever—the Spirit of truth, whom the world cannot receive, because it neither sees Him nor knows Him; but you know Him, for He dwells with you and will be in you. I will not leave you orphans; I will come to you' " (John 14:16-18).**

Sometimes in class, as we discuss the refreshment, which comes through God's Spirit, I ask students, "Would two or three of you tell the class about the most delightful mountain stream you have seen in your travels or back-packing?" Several usually respond. If time permits, I tell about one of my own: "One time my wife and I took about fifteen academy students to Mirror Lake, at about 10,000 feet elevation, where we spent Sabbath before going on to the summit of Mount Whitney on Sunday. On the way down, after we passed Mirror Lake, we could see a mountain stream off to the right of the trail. It left a mental picture of refreshment we shall never forget."

"On the last day, that great day of the feast, Jesus stood and cried out, saying, 'If anyone thirsts, let him come to Me and drink. He who believes in Me, as the Scripture has said, out of his heart will flow rivers of living water' " (John 7:37, 38).

**Refreshed by the Spirit**

In the above passage Jesus compared the Spirit to "living water." The book *Christ's Object Lessons* adds a "leaping from rock to rock" illustration:

> The heart that receives the word of God . . . is like the mountain stream fed by unfailing springs, whose cool, sparkling waters leap from rock to rock, refreshing the weary, the thirsty, the heavy laden 130).

Over and over Bible writers refer to the Holy Spirit as refreshing. Through Hosea God says, " 'I will be like the dew to Israel' " (14:5). And again, "He will come to us like the rain, like the latter and former rain to the earth" (6:3).

Chapter 68 of *The Desire of Ages* contains much related to John 14–16. Luke 11:1-13 contains Christ's response to the disciples' request, " 'Lord, teach us to pray' " (Luke 11:1), and climaxes in verse 13 with a promise of the Holy Spirit. For those 13 verses the chapter in *Christ's Object Lessons* titled "Asking to Give" offers many useful insights. Note this:

> We must not only pray in Christ's name, but by the inspiration of the Holy Spirit. This explains what is meant when it is said that the Spirit "maketh intercession for us, with groanings which cannot be uttered." Rom. 8:26. Such prayer God delights to answer (147).

The author further declares:

> When with earnestness and intensity we breathe a prayer in the name of Christ, there is in that very intensity a pledge from God that He is about to answer our prayer "exceeding abundantly above all that we ask or think." Eph. 3:20 (ibid.).

The asking makes a tremendous difference! Andrew Murray sums it up this way in his book *The Ministry of Intercession,* in what he calls "one great law." "The whole ministration of the Spirit is ruled by one great law: God must give, we must ask" (13). In the context he adds, "The measure of God's giving the Spirit is our asking" (15).

**"Without limit"**

What would your life be like if God gave you the fullest possible measure of every spiritual blessing offered in His Word? Consider, for example, this promise: " 'If you then, being evil, know how to give good gifts to your children, how much more will your heavenly Father give the Holy Spirit to those who ask Him!' " (Luke 11:13).

As he told about Christ's earthly ministry, John wrote that God gave Jesus "the fullness of his Spirit" (3:34, TEV). A "measureless" amount, says the NEB. "Without limit," according to the NIV. Would you be delighted to be given a "measureless" amount of the Holy Spirit? What would you be like if God did that for you?

What benefits, for example, might you receive from a total distrust of self? How about a full measure of hatred for sin? Could you use more of what God offers in the way of brokenness and of repentance? Or of implicit trust in the cleansing power of Christ's blood?

**Praying "in the Spirit"**

Scripture speaks of praying "in the Spirit" (Romans 8:9). As I understand it, praying in the Spirit is praying with an awareness of the Holy Spirit's presence. This depends on faith—not feeling—though at times you may sense the Holy Spirit as very close.

Often my greatest awareness of the Holy Spirit's presence comes when I am out-of-doors. When Philip found Nathanael and invited him to come see Jesus, the Savior told him, " 'Before Philip called you, when you were under the fig tree, I saw you' " (John 1:48).

We too need outdoor locations where we can go to pray. In our Michigan backyard I find, not a fig tree, but Rose of Sharon trees, morning glories in bloom, or a redbud that shades a portion of lawn on hot summer days. For other spots, I sometimes go to a cornfield, or to a telescope about a half mile from campus.

Paul speaks of being "filled with the Spirit" (Ephesians 5:18). What's that like? While in college, and at times since, I have built basements, constructed fireplaces, and laid brick. Can construction or any other kind of work be a Spirit-filled experience?

Galatians 5:22, 23 mentions nine fruits of the Spirit—love, joy, peace, longsuffering, kindness, goodness, faithfulness, gentleness, and self-control. I see being filled with the Spirit the same as possessing the fruits of the Spirit. *To be Spirit-filled is to be filled with love. And joy. And peace. And self-control. And with each of the other qualities listed.*

Being Spirit-filled doesn't make a fool out of you. Rather, the Holy Spirit helps you act with compassion, in love, and with dignity. For maximum enjoyment of conversation with God and Christ, we need to welcome the Holy Spirit into every aspect of our life.

**Application**

- Something to pray about: "He [she] who loves Christ the most will do the greatest amount of good. There is no limit to the usefulness of the one who, by putting self aside, makes room for the working of the Holy Spirit upon his [her] heart, and lives a life wholly consecrated to God" (*The Desire of Ages,* 250, 251).

# 13

## Use the Bible as a Sword

**"Be sober, be vigilant, because your adversary the devil walks about like a roaring lion, seeking whom he may devour" (1 Peter 5:8).**

"I'm too young to die," thought Susan Groves, a twenty-five-year-old water-quality specialist, as a mountain lion clamped its teeth over her head and held her under the icy water in a stream near Cortez, New Mexico.

"She doesn't remember how she got out of the stream, but suddenly she found herself on the bank sitting on top of the lion," reported the December 15, 1995 issue of the South Bend *Tribune* (A3). "Her arm was rammed in its mouth." Groves had taken a water sample from a stream for the Animal-LaPlata water project when the mountain lion attacked her. "Parking near a bridge," the paper reported, "she climbed 14 feet down the embankment to a stream, and started sampling about 1:30 p.m."

Groves said, "I heard something moving along the bank above me but didn't pay much attention. Then I looked up, saw the lion and as soon as we made eye contact, it came down the embankment to me."

The paper reports, "Groves stayed in the water thinking the cat was just checking her out and would leave. When it didn't she started screaming and throwing chunks of ice at the lion. 'The lion followed right along with me and as I crossed under the bridge, I stumbled, went down in the icy water, filling both of my waders. That's when it sunk its teeth in my head and held me under.' She next remembers being on the bank on top of the cat with her arm in its mouth. 'Then I reached in my fishing vest, found a pair of forceps and started jabbing the lion in the eyes with them.' "

The lion struggled and got away. Groves managed to climb the bank to the road, got to her truck, and drove 7 miles for help. Two federal Animal Control officers used dogs, tracked the lion, and killed it. It appeared to be an old female—weighing about 60 pounds—about half what a healthy adult female would weigh (ibid.).

**Keep a cool head**

Paul speaks of God's Word as a sword (Hebrews 4:12). *The Message* paraphrase puts Hebrews 4:12 like this: "His powerful Word is sharp as a surgeon's scalpel, cutting through everything, whether doubt or defense. . . . Nothing and no one is impervious to God's Word."

"Keep a cool head," *The Message* paraphrase words the above text. "Stay alert. The Devil is poised to pounce, and would like nothing better than to catch you napping."

That's good advice. And you have something better than fishing forceps. That's the sword of God's Word. But your enemy is far stronger than an old female mountain lion.

Remember that you have a tremendous advantage when you open your Bible to Matthew 27, where the blood of Christ is mentioned five times. In addition, remind Satan of the blood shed at Christ's scourging, at the slamming down of the crown of thorns, and the actual Crucifixion. As we have brought out in chapter 6, Satan actually does "tremble and flee."

**God did it!**

David had thirty mighty men who developed great skill in the use of the literal sword. 1 Samuel 23 and 1 Chronicles 11 tell of some of their exploits. On one occasion Adino the Eznite found himself outnumbered 800 to 1 by the Philistines. That's some odds! Yet he won (2 Samuel 23:8)!

On another occasion the Philistines who attacked the Hebrews so outnumbered the latter that the entire Hebrew army retreated in fear. A mighty man named Eleazar grabbed his sword and turned back the entire Philistine horde (2 Samuel 23:9). In 2 Samuel 23, in telling about these victories, the author twice stated, "The Lord brought about a great victory" (2 Samuel 23:10-12).

Truly God did it!

Today Satan especially fears the sword of God's Word. The Lord gave victory to David's "mighty men." But with the sword of the Spirit—when that sword gets backed with the blood of Christ—you can become invincible to Satan's attacks.

At this point, let three promises increase your courage:

- The deliverance promise: "No test or temptation that comes your way is beyond the course of what others have had to face. All you need to remember is that God will never let you down; he'll never let you be pushed past your

limit; he'll always be there to help you come through it" (1 Corinthians 10:13, *The Message*).
- The as-your-days promise: " 'As your days, so shall your strength be' " (Deuteronomy 33:25).

For more encouragement: "The trial will not exceed the strength that shall be given us to bear it. Then let us take up our work just where we find it, believing that whatever may come, strength proportionate to the trial will be given" (*Steps to Christ,* 125).

**Application**

- Select one idea in this chapter that you find most helpful, and for a few days, morning or evening, or both, pray about it when you kneel at your bedside.

# 14

# Energize Your Health

**"Didn't you realize your body is a sacred place, the place of the Holy Spirit? . . . God owns the whole works. So let people see God in and through your body" (1 Corinthians 6;19,20, *The Message*).**

What relationship do you see between health and energy and effectiveness in prayer?

*Let people see God in your body.* That can be a powerful witness without you saying a word! It takes one thing: the fruit of the Spirit. That includes "self-control" (Galatians 5:23). That may be why "self-denial" has been called the first lesson a Christian must learn.

The main caption on an Andrews University bulletin board urged, "Take good care of your body. It's the only place you have to live." The rest of the bulletin board included these suggestions:

- Lots of grains.
- Fresh fruits and vegetables every day.
- Almost no junk foods.
- Save sex until marriage.
- Get adequate rest.
- No alcohol or tobacco.

Grandma Whitney, the woman who first climbed Mt. Whitney when she was sixty-six, and by ninety-one had climbed it twenty-three times, put it this way: "Take good care of your health—there's only one body per customer."

God and Jesus must have really enjoyed putting together the human body. In his book *The Gift,* Kim Johnson tells that Christ knelt down, took some clay and sand, and shaped Adam's body—the handsome face with its captivating eyes and bold forehead. Then He stood back, and grinned. In many ways Adam was like Himself. Jesus could hardly wait to breathe life into the body.

> Christ bent down again and placed His mouth onto the inanimate lips of the clay figure. He drew in a deep breath and slowly let it out. Suddenly healthy flesh appeared. The toes wiggled. The hands moved. The eyes opened and stared into the face of Christ. Adam smiled. Together they rose and hugged in a long, lingering embrace (135).

Next? "Expectantly Jesus soon fashioned another wonderful being, incorporating into her form a rib from man as a sign of closeness. Fully equal to Adam, Eve was molded with the very same care and exquisite attention to detail" (ibid.).

In late June of 2000, an article titled "Scientists Unlock Code," the South Bend *Tribune* reported a discovery that further revealed the exquisite nature of the human body. "Dubbing it 'The Book of Life,' scientists announced Monday that they had deciphered the human genetic code" (A1).

The paper cited Dr. Francis Collins—director of the National Human Genome Research Institute—as saying: "We have caught a glimpse of an instruction book previously known only to God." It also quoted our president as saying, "Today we are learning the language in which God created life. We are gaining ever more awe for the complexity, the beauty, the wonder of God's most divine and sacred gift" (ibid.).

A diagram in the *Tribune* showed that the nucleus of the human cell contains 23 pairs of chromosomes and that each chromosome contains "tightly coiled strands of DNA that would stretch out to about 6 feet long." The DNA contains billions of these base pairs. The genome has 3.1 billion sub-units (ibid.).

All this in a single cell! Your brain alone contains some ten billion cells! Each cell: 23 pairs of chromosomes. Each chromosome: coiled strands of DNA. Each DNA billions of genomes. Each genome: 3.1 billion parts.

"Thank you," David exclaimed, "for making me so wonderfully complex! It is amazing to think about. Your workmanship is marvelous" (Psalm 139:14, TLB).

> The mechanism of the human body . . . presents mysteries that baffle the most intelligent. . . . In God we live and move and have our being. The beating heart, the throbbing pulse, every nerve and muscle in the living organism, is kept in order and activity by the power of an ever-present God (*The Ministry of Healing,* 417).

The above holds true for every part of your body! Every organ, wonderfully complex! Every process—breathing, digestion, circulation, heartbeat, sleep, white corpuscles, distribution of oxygen—wonderfully complex.

**Liver.** "Biologists have spent much of the last century taking cells apart to figure out what makes them tick. . . . It's a daunting task. A single enzyme in a liver cell may be controlled by as many as 14 regulatory processes. Multiply that by thousands of interconnected chemical reactions operating simultaneously in billions of cells, and you've got one incredibly complex system" (*Time,* 7 August 2000, 75).

**Stem cells.** "Your body contains many types of stem cells. . . . Adult stem cells reproduce to renew various tissues as needed, such as 200 billion new red blood cells required by your body each day" (*Mayo Clinic Health Letter*, November 2000, 1).

**Blood.** Your heart normally pumps more than 5 quarts of blood every minute, 2,000 gallons a day. During great exertion—like running—it can pump up to 40 quarts a minute. In order to get blood with its life-giving oxygen and nutrients to every muscle and nerve, your heart-pump sends blood through 60,000 to 100,000 *miles* of blood vessels.

**Reproduction.** "It is one of life's most splendid mysteries: In nine months, a 0.025-inch fertilized egg somehow turns into a kicking, crying human baby. No topic could be more intriguing—or less understood. Humans start life small and inglorious, as 'little sluglike things,' says one developmental biologist. But the 'slug' somehow conjures up eyes, a brain, and other organs" (*U.S News*, 18 September 1995, 104).

**Caring for God's miracles**

In this age of junk food and high-fat foods, we may be tempted to eat lots of junk food. The best choice, with a lot of fruits and vegetables along with grains, is a vegetarian diet in which your goal is "the 10 percent solution" to heart attacks: reducing total fat intake to 10 percent of calories consumed.

Some estimate that 90 percent of our health problems result from poor food choices—and often those choices come from an appetite not under the control of Christ. Some put it: "You can dig your grave with your fork." Appetite, however, is not the enemy. It was given in Eden as a part of "very good" gifts (Genesis 1:29-31). Only when reason is uninformed, and/or not in control, does appetite become an enemy and a terrible curse.

Most needed for appetite control: a consuming love for Christ and a caring love for people that determines not to hurt family and friends by a sooner-than-necessary death (Matthew 22:37-39). Other health care factors include getting adequate rest, spending time in fresh air, exercising regularly, and trusting in divine power.

**Motivation!**

"You are not your own. . . . For you were bought at a price," the New King

James words our opening text. That purchase price: Christ's suffering and death on Calvary. What He went through we will never understand, even in eternity. The following will help:

- the chapter in *The Desire of Ages* entitled "Calvary"

What a price He paid! When tempted, remember Jesus on Calvary. Think of His hands, nailed to wooden bars for both of us.

- Kim Johnson's book *The Gift*

The first ten chapters contain descriptions of the various kinds of suffering Christ endured: Being misunderstood, physical torture, verbal abuse, forsaken by God, the scourgings, the physical pain on the cross, the pain of carrying the sins of the entire planet. Consider a single paragraph:

> Delighted to finally get his hands on Christ, the devil put the Lord through five trials, four brutal beatings, two flesh-destroying scourgings, and then the horrors of crucifixion. We can hardly imagine what Jesus must have felt as He was deserted by the One He had depended on since childhood as His best Friend, shield, and protector (117).

- The chapter in *Testimonies for the Church,* Volume 2, entitled "The Sufferings of Christ."

This is one of the first chapters that students in my "Introduction to the Testimonies" class read. I generally ask them to memorize this sentence: "The contemplation of the matchless depths of a Saviour's love should fill the mind, touch and melt the soul, refine and elevate the affections, and completely transform the whole character (213).

Do you desire that complete transformation? Here's a powerful "how to": "We need to keep ever before us the efficacy of the blood of Jesus" (*Our High Calling,* 47).

**Application**

- Re-read the last part of Leviticus 17:11, along with 1 Peter 1:18, 19, then review them before your bedside prayer tomorrow morning.

# 15

# Urge Principles God Gave

**" 'As your days, so shall your strength [wisdom] be' "**
**(Deuteronomy 33:25).**

This chapter outlines my discoveries about group intercessory prayer—particularly for prayer meetings. A text of Scripture and a Spirit of Prophecy statement support each of these discoveries. At the end of the chapter I've summarized my key ideas about prayer and prayer meetings in one-sentence statements.

**Why pray?**

"If any of you lacks wisdom, let him ask of God, who gives to all liberally and without reproach, and it will be given him" (James 1:5).

> It is a part of God's plan to grant us, in answer to the prayer of faith, that which He would not bestow did we not thus ask (*The Great Controversy,* 525).

**Helping children enjoy worship**

" 'And these words which I command you today shall be in your heart. You shall teach them diligently to your children' " (Deuteronomy 6:6, 7).

> In every family there should be a fixed time for morning and evening worship (*Child Guidance,* 520).

> Let the father select a portion of Scripture that is interesting and easily understood; a few verses will be sufficient to furnish a lesson which may be studied and practiced through the day. . . . At least a few verses of spirited

> song may be sung, and the prayer offered should be short and pointed (ibid., 522).

> Let the services be brief and full of life, . . . and varied from time to time. . . . It will add to the interest of the children if they are sometimes permitted to select the reading. Question them upon it, and let them ask questions. Mention anything that will serve to illustrate its meaning (ibid.).

**Prayer as a hedge**

" 'Have You not made a hedge about him, around his household, and around all that he has on every side?' " (Job 1:10).

> By sincere, earnest prayer parents should make a hedge about their children. They should pray with full faith that God will abide with them and that holy angels will guard them and their children from Satan's cruel power (*Testimonies for the Church,* 7:42, 43).

> In every Christian home God should be honored by the morning and evening sacrifices of prayer and praise. . . . It is the duty of Christian parents, morning and evening, by earnest prayer and persevering faith, to make a hedge about their children (*Counsels to Parents, Teachers, and Students,* 110).

> Build a fortification of prayer and faith about your children (*Testimonies,* 2:398).

**Too busy?**

" 'Were there not any found who returned to give glory to God except this foreigner?' " (Luke 17:18).

> In many homes, prayer is neglected. Parents feel they have no time for morning and evening worship. They cannot spare a few moments to be spent in thanksgiving to God for His abundant mercies,—for the blessed sunshine and the showers of rain, and for the guardianship of holy angels. They have no time to offer prayer for divine help and guidance, and for the abiding presence of Jesus in the household (*Review and Herald,* 23 December 1902).

> When you rise in the morning, kneel at your bedside, and ask God to give you strength to fulfill the duties of the day, and to meet its temptations. . . . Ask Him to help you speak words that will inspire those around you with hope and courage, and draw you nearer to the Saviour (*Sons and Daughters of God,* 199).

**Why prayer meetings?**

"He Himself gave . . . pastors and teachers, for the equipping of the saints for the work of ministry, for the edifying of the body of Christ" (Ephesians 4:11, 12).

> What is the object of assembling together? . . . We meet together to edify one another by an interchange of thoughts and feelings, to gather strength, and light, and courage by becoming acquainted with one another's hopes and aspirations; and by our earnest, heartfelt prayers, offered up in faith (*Testimonies,* 2:578).

Note: Ponder this summary as to *why* prayer meeting, and *how* each benefit might be gained? (1) *Edification of one another*—most readily provided by some kind of preaching or Bible study; (2) *enlightenment, strength, and courage*—most readily provided by a pastor's presentation; (3) *an interchange of thoughts and feelings*—some kind of testimony or testimonies, each no longer than three or four minutes; (4) *heartfelt prayer*—small groups of two or three, no prayer longer than a minute unless popcorn prayers (see pages 26, 83, 84) are used.

**Prayer does well to begin with praise**

"Let everything that has breath praise the Lord. Praise the Lord!" (Psalm 150:6). See also Psalm 98:1; Psalm 100; Psalm 101:1.

> We do not pray any too much, but we are too sparing in giving thanks. If the loving-kindness of God called forth more . . . praise, we would have more power in prayer (*Testimonies,* 5:317).

**Up-front or group prayers: Keep short**

Use the Lord's Prayer as a model for public prayer—less than a minute in length (Matthew 6:9-13).

> Christ impressed upon His disciples the idea that their prayers should be short, expressing just what they wanted, and no more. He gives the length and substance [sample content] of their prayers, expressing their desires for temporal and spiritual blessings, and their gratitude for the same. How comprehensive this sample prayer! . . . One or two minutes is long enough for any ordinary prayer (*Testimonies,* 2:581).

Note: Three words describe the Lord's Prayer: short, simple, sincere. It has six requests; three kingdom needs (God's name hallowed, His kingdom come, His will be done); and three personal needs (daily bread, forgiveness, deliverance). Both the start and the ending reflect praise.

**Speak clearly and distinctly**

"So they read distinctly from the book . . . and they gave the sense, and helped them to understand the reading" (Nehemiah 8:8).

> Let those who pray and those who speak pronounce their words properly and speak in clear, distinct, even tones. . . . Satan rejoices when the prayers offered to God are almost inaudible. . . . Let the testimonies borne and the prayers offered be clear and distinct (*Testimonies,* 6:382).

Note: Repeatedly the Spirit of Prophecy urges that prayers be audible, clear, and distinct. Don't mumble. Don't speak into your hands. Don't bow so low you can't be heard. And in length, it's better to be too short rather than too long. Nothing kills prayer meeting like a lengthy, mumbled prayer.

**During prayer, don't sermonize**

For public prayers see the Lord's Prayer, 2 Chronicles 20:6-12; Acts 4:24-30. For examples of private prayer see John 17; Philippians 1:9-11; Ephesians 3:14-19.

> Many offer prayer in a dry, sermonizing manner . . . they deliver a discourse. . . . All such prayers . . . are made of no account of in heaven. Angels of God are wearied with them, as well as mortals who are compelled to listen to them (*Testimonies,* 2:581, 582).

> Secret prayer is neglected, and this is why many offer such long, tedious, backslidden prayers when they assemble to worship God (*Testimonies,* 2:582).

> When you pray, be brief, come right to the point. Do not preach the Lord a sermon in your long prayers (*Testimonies,* 5:201).

**Make prayer meeting the "most interesting" of all sessions**

"So Judah gathered together to ask help from the Lord; and from all the cities of Judah they came to seek the Lord. . . . All Judah, with their little ones, their wives, and their children" (2 Chronicles 20:4, 13).

> Everything possible should be done to make the meetings of our people interesting. . . . Especially should our social meetings [prayer meetings] be properly conducted (*Testimonies,* 4:133).

> These meetings should be most precious seasons and should be made interesting to all who have any relish for religious things (*Testimonies,* 2:578).

Note: *Made* most interesting! If we had lived in Judah, facing slaughter from three heathen nations, and our king called a prayer session to "seek the Lord," wouldn't we show up? Even the children! Even the little ones!

If church folk find the "bread of life" at the prayer meeting they will be there to receive it. Does not that suggest that along with opportunities for prayer, people expect and need some preaching and/or Bible study?

**Seek a present blessing—for those present**

"These all continued with one accord in prayer and supplication" (Acts 1:14).

> When in the house of God, we should pray for a present blessing and should expect God to hear and answer our prayers. Such meetings will be lively and interesting (*Testimonies,* 1:146).

> Let the soul go out after God with intense longing for the blessing needed at that time (*Testimonies,* 5:201).

**Spirit-filled sessions**

"Be filled with the Spirit" (Ephesians 5:18).

> Let the Spirit of God into your hearts, and it will sweep away all dry formality (*Testimonies,* 4:71).

> Fervent and effectual prayer is always in place, and will never weary. Such prayer interests and refreshes all who have a love for devotion (*Testimonies,* 2:582).

> Go to your Saviour in faith, tell Him what you need on that occasion. Let the soul go out after God with intense longing for the blessing needed at that time (*Testimonies,* 5:201).

Note: Does not the above refreshing of the weary, the thirsty, the heavy laden, imply some preaching on prayer-meeting night? Prayer groups, if Spirit-filled, can bless the weary, but don't the thirsty and heavy laden need a presentation from God's Word?

**Spirit-filled singing also helps**

Singing the psalms added much to temple worship. Many psalms, in fact, were written to be set to music.

> Music can be a great power for good, yet we do not make the most of this branch of worship. . . . Music should have beauty, pathos, and power. Let the voices be lifted in songs of praise and devotion. Call to your aid, if

practicable, instrumental music, and let the glorious harmony ascend to God (*Testimonies,* 4:71).

Note: For sake of attendance by children, and their parents, pastors and parents could consider regularly having a children's choir, and at other times, a choir of teens.

**Prayer groups: Keep small**

Much of Christ's guidance was given to twelve men—His family. New Testament house churches began as small groups: Jason's house in Thessalonica (Acts 17:5-7); Justus's home in Corinth (Acts 18:7, 8, NKJV); the house of Nymphas (Colossians 4:15); the house of Priscilla and Aquila (Romans 16:3-5). Most likely, each began as a small group.

Note: The Teen Prayer Conference movement, which uses small groups of ten to twelve people, have found small groups effective both for prayer and for Bible study. Both at Southwestern College in the fall of 1997, when 600 teens from North America attended, and in the fall of 1998, when 800 attended a similar Teen Prayer Conference at the Pioneer Memorial Church, at Andrews University, these groups met four to five times, with the same students to the same groups each time.

**Prayer in groups**

" 'Where two or three are gathered together in My name, I am there in the midst of them' " (Matthew 18:20).

> Why do not two or three meet together and plead with God for the salvation of some special one, and then for still another? . . . The formation of small companies as a basis of Christian effort has been presented to me by One who cannot err. If here is a large number in the church, let the members be formed into small companies, to work not only for the church members, but for unbelievers (*Testimonies,* 6:21, 22).

Note: For many excellent ideas, see entire article, titled "Work for Church Members." The "meet together" for the most part would be outside of prayer meetings, but many suggestions would also fit for organizing prayer groups at prayer meeting.

**Shun indistinct, mumbled prayers**

"So they read [prayed] distinctly . . . and helped them to understand the reading" (Nehemiah 8:8).

> Let those who pray and those who speak pronounce their words properly and speak in clear, distinct, even tones. . . . Satan rejoices when the prayers offered to God are almost inaudible. . . . Let the testimonies borne and the prayers offered be clear and distinct (*Testimonies,* 6:382).

**Ten munites maximum length for public kneeling**

I am not aware of any Bible statement that mentions length for kneeling, but the Lord's Prayer and other public prayers in the Bible give examples. With common sense Ellen White suggested:

> From the light I have had upon the subject I have decided that God does not require us, as we assemble for His worship, to make these seasons tedious and wearisome by remaining bowed quite a length of time, listening to several long prayers (*Testimonies,* 2:577).

> Upon common occasions there should not be prayer of more than ten minutes' duration. After there has been a change of position, and the exercise of singing or exhortation has relieved the sameness, then, if any feel the burden of prayer, let them pray (*Testimonies,* 2:578).

**Private prayer: As long as one wishes**

The Bible has two recorded prayers of Jesus—the Lord's Prayer (Matthew 6, and a later version Luke 11) and His John 17 prayer. The latter is the longer of the two, but of course, some of His prayers may not be recorded. At times Jesus prayed for hours, even all night.

> Long, prosy talks and prayers are out of place anywhere, and especially in the social [prayer] meeting. Those who are forward and ever ready to speak are allowed to crowd out the testimony of the timid and retiring. Those who are the most superficial generally have the most to say. Their prayers are long and mechanical. They weary the angels and the people who listen to them. Our prayers should be short and right to the point. Let the long, tiresome petitions be left for the closet, if any have such to offer (*Testimonies,* 4:70, 71).

**Family requests: Pray in private**

These may be mentioned, as doubtless happened in the Acts 1 prayer sessions. But the burden was getting the gospel proclamation started. Note this:

> We should not come to the house of God to pray for our families unless deep feeling shall lead us while the Spirit of God is convicting them. Generally, the proper place to pray for our families is at the family altar (*Testimonies,* 1:145).

**Non-present people: Pray for at home**

Exceptions could arise, but here, again, Acts 1 could be an example. With 120 in the upper room, the first priority must have been oneness with each other.

> When the subjects of our prayers are at a distance, the closet is the proper place to plead with God for them (*Testimonies,* 1:146).

Note: Does the following imply possible exceptions? "We should not come to the house of God to pray for our families *unless* feeling shall lead us while the Spirit of God is convicting them. Generally, the proper place to pray for our families is at the family altar" (*Testimonies,* 1:145, emphasis supplied).

**Application**

- Discuss the ideas in this summary chapter with one other person or in a small group.
- Do all you can to be present at every mid-week, ready to briefly testify of your own experience, or some witness you gave.

**Sentence summaries**

1. Prayer does well to begin with praise.
2. Formal, wordy prayers distress God.
3. Maximum prayer length in public: one or two minutes.
4. Public or private, never sermonize God.
5. Long public prayers weary the angels.
6. Lengthy prayers: only in private, in closet.
7. Meeting attendance takes much that attracts.
8. A promise from *Testimonies* (4:70): If bread of life is offered, people will come—this implies some preaching.
9. Above takes much planning and forethought.
10. Make provision for children, youth, students.
11. Spirit-filled music adds much.
12. At times use a children's choir at prayer meeting.
13. At prayer meeting, pray for a *present* blessing.
14. On Sabbath let people know *what* prayer meetings offer.
15. Repeatedly let people know *why* prayer meeting matters.
16. Prayer-meeting attendance and the latter rain go together.
17. Spirit of God at prayer meeting sweeps away dry formality.
18. Relatives: pray for at home—not at church.
19. People not present: pray for at home—not at church.
20. Don't let talkative ones monopolize testimonies.
21. Encourage shy ones to pray, and to testify.
22. Encourage those who witness to testify, but keep brief.
23. Every sincere prayer, private or public, does good.
24. Each such prayer goes into the book of remembrance.

# 16

# Start With Telephone or Email

**" 'But you, Daniel, shut up the words, and seal the book, until the time of the end. Many shall run to and fro, and knowledge shall increase' " (Daniel 12:4, RSV).**

More than a decade ago, someone used this illustration: let all the technical knowledge for the first 1950 years since the time of Christ be represented by an eight-inch graph—height of a Sabbath School quarterly. The knowledge from the first two decades since 1950 would take a graph as high as a twenty-story building. And of the three decades since then? No building on earth would be high enough!

What's behind all this increase of knowledge? Like the telephone and like email, for example?

I want to tell you about Clifford, of Tacoma Park, Maryland. At the age of three he had a playmate whose parents went to a Seventh-day Adventist Church. From that playmate Clifford knew about the Sabbath. That planted a seed in his mind. His parents, though not regular church attendees, went to a Methodist church. At fifteen, one day as he rode a bus, another passenger gave him a *Happiness Digest,* and urged him to read it.

Clifford opened it. "It seemed like beams of light came from that book," he later said. But "I'm not interested in that," he told himself, and threw it on the floor.

The giver of the book must have prayed. Before long Clifford hunted up a Seventh-day Adventist church. "Two things attracted me," he said. "They kept the Bible Sabbath, and the people were so friendly." At sixteen he was baptized. About a year later his dad also joined the same church. For a time Clifford attended college at Oakwood, then he came to Andrews. I met him at the cafeteria and sometimes he attended an early morning prayer group that I and others sponsored.

**Prayer by phone**

At the time of this writing, he does not attend school but keeps in touch by telephone. He calls several times a week, mostly to pray. His prayers are brief, and I too keep them to about thirty seconds.

Over the last six or eight months, we have prayed together scores, maybe hundreds of times. When I ask him for his requests, his most frequent ones are as follows, though never all at one time. One, or two at the most, for a specific time.

- for the Holy Spirit for himself
- for the Holy Spirit and unity for the church
- for the righteousness of Jesus
- for the latter rain

I share this with the hope that hundreds of telephone prayer partners will result. I personally pray fairly often with a retired academy Bible teacher. If you do form a telephone partnership for prayer, I suggest prayers never longer than a minute or two each.

- Keep it someone of the same sex.
- If you are a retiree, get at least one retiree as a partner.
- Share one or two requests before you pray.
- Both of you keep your prayers to less than a minute each.
- Regularly pray for at least one or two Christian schools.

Praying together has a bonding effect that can sometimes produce unwanted effects between a man and a woman. Billy Graham, I've heard, told ministers in training to never be alone with one person of the opposite sex.

If you can, find a retired person you can pray with by telephone. Our church would gain great blessing from the elderly who imitate the example of Anna, of whom the Bible says: "This woman was a widow of about eighty-four years, who did not depart from the temple, but served God with fastings and prayers night and day" (Luke 2:37).

Anna evidently prayed alone, but could Sabbaths also be a time when two or three women or two or three men go apart to pray together, but keeping prayers quite brief? See especially the chapter entitled "Pray Jabez Prayers." That prayer has much potential as you pray for yourself and other older folk.

**Inviting God to work**

The greatest blessing in telephone praying comes from inviting God to work. Someone has said, *"When we work, we work, but when we pray, God works."* For an example we turn to Exodus 17. The Amalakites, descendants of Esau, repeatedly fought against the Hebrews. In the days of Queen Esther, for example, an Amalakite named Haman attempted to destroy all Jews in Persia. As Moses and the Hebrews went toward Sinai, Amalakite warriors attempted to wipe out the ones at the rear, especially the more elderly or feeble.

On this occasion Moses asked Joshua to take a group of young men out to fight the attackers. In his book *Joshua,* W. Philip Keller comments:

> This was no easy assignment. Joshua was not a military commander. Like his companions he had spent his young life in the slime pits of Egypt making bricks for Pharaoh. His battle experience was nil. . . . It was a bloodbath that raged back and forth all day in the hot sun. Men fell on both sides, their lifeblood spilling out from ghastly sword wounds to stain the desert sands and stones (18, 19).

As Moses held his hands up in prayer, the Amalakites retreated. But when his arms grew weary and dropped, Aaron and Hur—who had accompanied Moses—noticed that the Amalakites pushed forward. They seated Moses on a rock and held up his hands as he prayed. Again the Hebrews prevailed.

Could the latter rain—a Pentecostal descent of the Holy Spirit—largely depend on whether or not you and I take the above truth and start calling on the Lord, like we never have in all our history as the Advent movement?

**When a person prays**

In Isaiah 37 these words to Hezekiah stand out: " ' "Because you have prayed" ' " (v. 21). Consider other examples.

- " 'At the beginning of your supplications the command went out, and I have come to tell you' " (Daniel 9:23).

Daniel had seen things in a vision of chapter 8 that he did not understand. Before giving an explanation in Daniel 9, Gabriel told Daniel that he had come because of the prophet's prayers.

- " 'I have come because of your words' " (Daniel 10:12).

Before saying this, the angel had told Daniel, " 'From the first day that you set your heart to understand, and to humble yourself before your God, your words were heard' " (Daniel 10:12).

**Application**

- Make requests for God's Spirit, and for revival, as top priority in your praying. Prophecy has anticipated, at the end time, a revival of Bible study and a revival of earnest intercession.

# 17

## Ask Forgiveness for All

**" 'Father, forgive them, for they do not know what they do' " (Luke 23:34).**

In his *Incredible Answers to Prayer* and in *Incredible Power of Prayer,* and also in a video about this subject, Roger Morneau urged that as we pray for others, the first thing to ask is: "Father, please forgive their sins."

I sometimes find youth and others who question this idea of asking forgiveness in behalf of those who do not yet feel any need for God or for His forgiveness. I generally refer them to Christ's example as given in our opening text. But let me also refer to this comment in *The Desire of Ages:*

> Some of them would yet see their sin, and repent, and be converted. Some by their impenitence would make it an impossibility for the prayer of Christ to be answered for them. Yet, just the same, God's purpose was reaching its fulfillment. Jesus was earning the right to become the advocate of men in the Father's presence.
>
> That prayer of Christ for His enemies embraced the world. It took in every sinner that had lived or should live, from the beginning of the world to the end of time. Upon all rests the guilt of crucifying the Son of God. To all, forgiveness is freely offered. "Whosoever will" may have peace with God, and inherit eternal life (745).

In his video, Roger Morneau suggests that the following are needed for effective intercessory prayer:

- First, ask God to forgive the sins of the person for whom you are praying.

- Ask that the person be surrounded by God's Holy Spirit—with a sense of the Holy Spirit's presence and the peace that it can bring.
- Claim the blood of Calvary in that person's behalf.

For the latter Mr. Morneau suggests that we open our Bible to Matthew 27:45-65, and mentally take a journey from Pilate's judgment hall to Calvary. He does this, he says, before presenting his requests.

**What a Savior!**

One of my greatest teaching privileges has been that of a class we call "Introduction to the Testimonies." For this, we go through the set one volume at a time. The syllabus contains selected quotes from each of the first six volumes. This morning, late November of 2000, we started through the quotes for volume 5 . From the chapter titled "Laborers for God," the syllabus included this sentence about Jesus: "So devoted was our Redeemer to the work of saving souls that He even longed for His baptism of blood" (132).

Incredible! I asked myself, "How could Jesus actually long for intense pain, for indescribable suffering? The only answer? Love. Love for you, love for me, love for every person, even those who say "No" to Him.

We can only exclaim, "What a Savior!"

**Back to His departure**

Matthew tells that after His resurrection, Jesus went to a mountain in Galilee, and met with the believers. "When they saw Him, they worshipped Him; but some doubted" (28:17). *The Message* paraphrase gives the passage this way: "Some, though, held back, not sure . . . about risking themselves totally." Jesus, undeterred, went right ahead and sent them out to make other disciples. And He said, " 'I'll be with you as you do this, day after day after day, right up to the end of the age.' "

I cite this because of the expression *day after day after day.*

That's the way Jesus has been with everything, and with His ongoing offer of forgiveness. Shall we not thank Him for that graciousness? You can count on forgiveness *day after day after day.* To which He adds, "I'll also be with you *day after day after day.*"

In Workshop in Prayer, we just finished underlining promises in Galatians through Colossians. As we discussed Colossians 2:10, "You are complete in Him," I reminded the class what that includes, as expressed in an *Education* comment, which I cited: "Through faith in Christ, every deficiency of character may be supplied, every defilement cleansed, every fault corrected, every excellence developed" (257). I then listed these four things available through Jesus:

- every deficiency of character supplied
- every defilement cleansed

- every fault corrected
- every excellence developed

I asked the class to prayerfully evaluate all four, and if one was special reason for gratitude, to write two or three sentences about it. With permission, I share what one young man wrote:

> For me the most important one is to be cleansed of defilement. Sin is a part of me; it courses through my veins, controls my thoughts, and determines what I do. We are all defiled, corrupted, and just plain dirty. I pray God to let me see more clearly my nature, lest I think, "I'm not so bad." I wallow in my own filth, in the things that lead to death.

At times do you, too, sense your awfulness? May I direct you to Romans 8? God used Paul in that chapter—one that mentioned the Holy Spirit five times, with one verse declaring: "Likewise the Spirit also helps in our weaknesses. For we do not know what we should pray for as we ought, but the Spirit Himself makes intercession for us with groanings which cannot be uttered" (v. 26).

**Keeping up-to-date**

Here's an idea from Dick Eastman's *The Hour that Changes the World.* In the chapter "Confession—the Act of Admission" he includes a suggestion about keeping up-to-date: "Often a quick mental trip through the previous twenty-four hours reveals need for confession" (47).

For that mental trip, journaling can help. During my morning devotions, I take a half sheet of typing paper, and on one side, along with the date, write "Yesterday." I then record key events of yesterday, and also any sins needing confession. I then use the other side for prayer requests, and for a record of new insights discovered.

Eastman suggests:

- Keep your own need for cleansing and forgiveness current.
- When you pray for someone, first of all ask that God forgive their sins.

**Application**

- As your first step in intercessory prayer, Roger Morneau suggests you ask forgiveness for the person for whom you intercede.
- Does that make sense to you? You may want to discuss this with a friend.
- If you have access to the book *Education,* you may want to prayerfully study the context for the sentence on page 257 cited in this chapter.

# 18

## Pray Jabez Prayers

### (For Yourself and Others)

**" 'Oh, that You would bless me indeed, and enlarge my territory [influence], that Your hand would be with me, and that You would keep me from evil' " (1 Chronicles 4:10).**

In *The Prayer of Jabez* Bruce Wilkinson asks: "What if you found out that God had in mind to send you twenty-three specific blessings today, but you got only one? What do you suppose the reason would be?" (25).

Wilkinson then relates what he calls "a little fable." A Mr. Jones dies, goes to heaven, and at the gate Peter greets him. The apostle gives him a tour that takes in the golden streets, the mansions, and other wonders. Mr. Jones notices a building that looks like an enormous warehouse. It has no windows and only one door. Mr. Jones asks to see inside. Peter hesitates, saying, "You really don't want to see what's in there."

As the tour ends, Jones still wonders. He asks again and Peter reluctantly opens the door. Mr. Jones almost knocks him over in his haste to see. It turns out the enormous building is filled with row after row of shelves, floor to ceiling, each stacked with white boxes tied with red ribbons. Mr. Jones notes that each box has a name on it. He turns to Peter and asks, "Do I have one?"

"Yes, you do," Peter replies as he tries to guide Mr. Jones back outside. But Mr. Jones has dashed toward the "J" aisle to find his box.

Peter, shaking his head, catches up with Mr. Jones just as he slips the red ribbon off his box. As Jones looks inside, he lets out a deep sigh. In his box are all the blessings God wanted to give him while he was on earth. But Jones never asked (ibid., 27).

**"Living Great for God"**

At this point I want to recommend Bruce Wilkinson's book *The Prayer of Jabez,* which you can probably get or order from any Christian bookstore (published by Multnomah, Box 1720, Sisters, OR, 97759). Pastor Dwight Nelson did a five-part series based on that book during the summer of 2000. By the second presentation, the Andrews bookstore had sold 500 copies. The local ABC also carried it, and by the end of the summer the two places had sold over 1,000 copies.

Note these words in my title for this chapter: "For yourself and others." Just as Jesus did in John 17, pray for yourself first, then expand your prayers to take in others, youth in particular. I sent a copy of this book to several people, one of which was a brother in a Denver suburb. He shared it with the church he attends, the Littleton, Colorado SDA Church. Later he told me that some fifty members at that church had gotten a copy, and that an SDA pastor at another Denver church who had seen it intended to promote it to his congregation.

I recommend Wilkinson's chapter based on this prayer of Jabez: "O that you would enlarge my territory." Wilkinson titled his chapter "Living Large for God," in which he rephrased the request of Jabez this way: *"O God and King, please expand my opportunities and my impact in such a way that I touch more lives for Your glory. Let me do more for You"* (32).

**Praying for Adventist Youth**

I sent the above book to a Carol Davidson, a student from Washington state who attended the 1998-99 college school year at Southern University, and whom I had gotten acquainted with through a Prayer Conference and her Berrien Springs grandparents. At the time I sent it (June 2000) she was leading a group of Academy youth in selling magabooks in a suburb of Seattle.

Her grandparents said that at the time she finished *The Prayer of Jabez,* she asked her academy youth to join her in praying for a $2,000 week. She had especially liked Wilkinson's chapter "Living Great for God." Up to this time their best weeks had been $1,000 totals. Carol and her group prayed, "Lord, help us this week to sell $2,000 in message books." Through God's blessing they did!

Does this Joel 2 prophecy indicate God has His eyes upon youth as recipients of His Spirit?

> "And it shall come to pass afterward that I will pour out My Spirit on all flesh; your sons and your daughters shall prophesy, your old men shall dream dreams, your young men shall see visions. And also on My menservants and on My maidservants I will pour out My Spirit in those days" (Joel 2:28, 29).

Note six groups mentioned in this promise: sons, daughters, old men, young men, menservants, maidservants. All of us, of course, are sons or daughters. But of the other four groups, wouldn't three of the four be mostly under thirty? Would not menservants or maidservants generally be younger folk? I see the following: We can expect youth—people under thirty—to be a prominent part of the repentance described in Joel 2:12-17.

**Getting fervent about prayer**

My family and I moved near the Andrews University campus in 1970 so I could assist with the development of new religion books for Adventist academies. While writing I wanted to keep in touch with students, and in 1972 I asked for and got permission to teach a college undergraduate class in which we would study faith and prayer. Seven students enrolled the first time I taught it, but as I continued teaching it sometimes up to fifty or more would take the class.

Almost every year since I have taught a "Workshop in Prayer" class at Andrews University. The two Bible texts that led me to develop a class about prayer were: " 'Lord, teach us to pray' " (Luke 11:1) and "Lord, 'Increase our faith' " (Luke 17:5).

I had also read a chapter in the book *Education* entitled "Faith and Prayer." There the author suggests:

> Prayer and faith are closely allied, and they need to be studied together. In the prayer of faith there is a divine science; it is a science that everyone who would make his lifework a success must understand (257).

That got my attention! There's a "divine science" in the prayer of faith—and *it's a science that everyone who would make his lifework a success must understand!* The study of faith and prayer is not just for religion majors and pastors. It's for every person who wants to succeed in life. And it applies just as much to those in the work world as it does to youth still in school.

Why is prayer called a "science"? Isn't it because, like in chemistry, it's governed by laws? Through understanding and praying in harmony with those laws, or conditions, our answers to prayer markedly increase. (On this the chapter in *Steps to Christ* titled "The Privilege of Prayer" concisely reviews conditions for getting answers to prayer.)

**A degree in prayer?**

You can get a degree in every area of physical science that exists. Shouldn't that be true of the science of prayer?

During the middle 1970s, the seminary allowed me to teach a class for seminarians under the title "The Ministry of Prayer"—a practice I continued for about six quarters. When publishing deadlines made it necessary to drop part of my teaching, I continued only with the undergraduate course.

I read somewhere about a seminary at which students could get a degree in prayer. Doesn't a need for such courses become more and more urgent? Should our colleges and universities and the Andrews Theological Seminary have enough courses on faith and prayer that they could offer some kind of degree in the science of prayer? Should a seminarian be able to take courses that would enable him to teach the science of prayer to his church members?

As we think about helping youth learn to pray, note this: "The eyes of the Lord range through the whole earth [KJV: run to and fro throughout the whole earth], to bring aid and comfort to those whose hearts are loyal to him" (2 Chronicles 16:9, NEB). Allow me to use a really striking comment about success that comes from *Counsels to Parents, Teachers, and Students.* (Note the full title includes both parents and students.) The comment:

> Upon the mind of every student should be impressed the thought that education is a failure unless the understanding has learned to grasp the truths of divine revelation, and unless the heart accepts the teachings of the gospel of Christ (12, 13).

*Education is a failure unless!* Maybe we indeed need to make sure every student learns to become Spirit-filled!

**Application**

- Memorize the bold print prayer that begins this chapter. Make it a daily request for yourself.
- Prayerfully read, maybe even memorize, the previous summary as to what "every student" needs to realize.

# 19

# Show Up Eagerly at Midweek Services

**" ' "Fear not, for I am with you; be not dismayed, for I am your God. I will strengthen you, yes, I will help you, I will uphold you with My righteous right hand" ' " (Isaiah 41:10).**

During my work on this book, time and again God has led to a possible illustration. That happened for this chapter. On the Saturday evening after Thanksgiving 2000, my wife and I had our family and their children at our home for Saturday night supper.

A son and daughter-in-law invited Randy and two of his children to join us. As we visited, I mentioned to Randy, a teacher at Andrews University, the text from Zechariah 10 and a quote about the Holy Spirit we used in chapter 2. He especially liked this quote—something totally new to him:

> The revenue of glory has been accumulating for this closing work of the third angel's message. Of the prayers that have been ascending for the fulfillment of the promise—the descent of the Holy Spirit—not one has been lost. Each prayer has been accumulating, ready to overflow and pour forth a healing flood of heavenly influence and accumulated light all over the world (*Manuscript Releases,* 21:155).

I asked about prayer meeting. He said, "The prayer meetings at my church, along with a mission trip that the church took, completely changed my life."

"What did the pastor talk about?" I asked.

"He went through *Thoughts From the Mount of Blessing,*" Randy replied. "For a time," he added, "we had a potluck at the church on Wednesday evenings just before the meeting. At other times we met at a member's home, but the potluck increased attendance." When I asked about that, he mentioned that about one-third of their 100 members came.

His church has many children. "Would it help to have Pathfinders on the same night as prayer meeting?" I asked. He said the board had discussed that, but decided against it. Randy then mentioned William Miller, of the 1844 movement, and his meetings. "Miller really knew his Bible, and as he talked, children also learned. I think that gives a key—if the speaker really uses the Bible, children can benefit too."

**Context for the latter rain quote**

The above quote about an "accumulating revenue" comes from a letter Ellen White wrote from her Sunnyside home in Australia, in 1899. The letter—titled "The Need for Faith, Love, and Christlikeness"—went to a Mrs. S.M.I. Henry—an early leader of the Woman's Christian Temperance Union. The *Seventh-day Adventist Encyclopedia* tells the following about Mrs. Henry (581, 582).

- born to an Illinois Methodist minister, frail in her childhood, married in 1861, and left with three children when her husband died ten years later
- supported her family by writing and teaching
- appalled that a son went to a saloon, which led her to organize the Christian women of Rockford, Illinois into a union
- gradually became a national evangelist for the WCTU
- became ill with a heart ailment, went to Battle Creek Sanitarium, became an Adventist in 1896, healed while in prayer

The letter to Mrs. Henry about faith, love, and Christlikeness contains several striking statements about God's work. Some I cite in class as a reminder of what God has in mind for this movement:

- The barren places of earth will become as the garden of the Lord (*Manuscript Releases,* 21:155).
- The meek shall be as David, and David as the angel of the Lord (ibid.).
- Every Christian will see in the face of every other the face of God in benevolence and brotherly love (ibid.).

Speaking to Mrs. Henry, Ellen White wrote of what happened at Pentecost early rain, at which time the Spirit of Christ animated the community of believers.

- Every pulse beat in concert (ibid., 156).
- One subject of emulation swallowed up every other. Who should approach nearest the likeness of Christ? Who should do most to glorify God? (ibid.).

Both there and at other times Ellen White spoke of what hindered the latter rain: "The church is too much, altogether too much, like the world; therefore the light is not reflected from them to the world" (ibid.), and "In order to represent Christ we must be strong in His strength, pure as He is pure; truth as it is in Jesus is planted in the heart" (ibid.).

Chapter 21 of this book—mostly about solving our rising curse of divorce—gives more ideas about experiencing the purity found in Jesus.

**Prayer meeting and the Spirit**

The closing part of chapter 2 gave really stirring reasons why we should never miss prayer meeting. Let me again ask two questions:

- Do you see why every prayer-meeting night should include prayers for the descent of the Holy Spirit?
- Do you understand why your prayers can change history?

To the above, I add this: Do you see why this book has put a major emphasis on attending the prayer meeting at your church? And if you are a pastor, do you see why every pastor, every leader, needs to urge attendance at prayer meeting?

Surely God dreams that the time will come when there will be as many present for prayer meeting night as attend on Sabbath morning. Surely Jesus never forgets what He said about the Holy Spirit in Luke 11! Nor does He forget this truth: "It is a part of God's plan to grant us, in answer to the prayer of faith, that which He would not bestow did we not thus ask" (*The Great Controversy,* 525).

If a parent or leader or pastor, ask yourself this question from chapter 2: "Isn't it time for the book of remembrance (Malachi 3:16) to be filled with hundreds and thousands of such requests?" Let's never forget the latter rain promises of Zechariah 10: "Ask the Lord for rain in the time of the latter rain. The Lord will make flashing clouds; He will give them showers of rain" (Zechariah 10:1). Until chapter and verse divisions were added, chapter 10 and the closing verse of Zechariah 9 made one passage. Of youth verse 17 says: "The Lord their God will save them in that day as the flock of his people. They will sparkle in his land like jewels in a crown. How attractive and beautiful they will be" (NIV).

Doesn't that provide subject matter for prayer?

**When large groups pray**

Suppose you get hundreds or even a thousand on a prayer-meeting night. In God's providence I attended parts of a prayer conference conducted by the Lake Union Education Department in September of 2000. This conference brought together 150 teens from the Lake Union. At the main meeting on Friday morning all 150 teens participated in a 90-minute session. It began with forty minutes of powerful preaching, followed by another fifty minutes for a group prayer session that consisted of prayers by both adults and teens.

For the prayer time the speaker asked all—teens or sponsors alike—to be seated or kneel on the platform or carpet at the front of the Youth Chapel. No prayers longer than one sentence, but a person could pray more than once. All would be spontaneous—no set order. At times anyone who wished could lead into a chorus, or read a verse of Scripture. The 50 minutes passed quickly. Several, teens and adults alike, made comments afterwards to this effect:

- "I sensed God's presence."
- "It seemed like God Himself was in that chapel."
- "What a blessing!"

As you already know, chapter 15 of this book, contains numerous Bible statements, mostly about Bible meetings and/or prayers. To close this chapter, let me ask two questions and suggest some answers based on my discoveries listed in chapter 15:

1. Why such a low attendance at midweek?
- Our lukewarmness. In chapter 29, we will look at possible solutions.
- In too many churches the Holy Spirit and latter rain have not been priority topics.
- Lengthy, tedious public prayers that weary humans, angels, and God Himself.
- Feeling of unworthiness, timidity.

2. What can elders, pastors, and parents do to increase an interest in private and group intercession for others?
- Really pray, remembering the law that in order to interest a child, a student, a fellow believer in the Bible and prayer, you must model a vivid interest yourself.
- As far as possible, keep idolatry out of your home, school, and church.
- With all up-front prayers, and all small group prayers, encourage—educate people, *require* that all be brief—no prayer longer than sixty to ninety seconds. If the pray-er errs at all, err by being too brief rather than too long.

**Application**
- Compare this chapter with chapter 5.
- Re-read the section "When large groups pray." See if somehow your church can get a group of 50 to 150 people together, with your pastor or an elder leading out, and try the method used for the 150 Lake Union teens.

# 20

# Treasure Repentance and Revival

**“ ‘If you keep the Sabbath holy,’ ” God told them, “ ‘not having your own fun and business on that day, but enjoying the Sabbath, and speaking of it with delight as the Lord’s holy day, and honoring the Lord in what you do, not following your own desires and pleasure nor talking idly—then the Lord will be your delight, and I will see to it that you ride high and get your full share of the blessings I promised to Jacob, your father.’ The Lord has spoken” (Isaiah 58:13, 14, TLB).**

Note the condition for getting a “full share” of God’s blessings: delight in God and in His Sabbath. That delight excludes secular business, games, and conversation on Sabbath.

Heaven’s “full share of blessings” was repeatedly promised to Israel in Deuteronomy. One blessing: that everything “might be well” both with individual families and with the entire nation. In Deuteronomy 5, God had Moses give the Ten Commandments a second time to the people. Moses then told the people about God’s heart-longing in Exodus 19 when they had promised to obey. “ ‘ “Oh, that they had such a heart in them that they would fear Me and always keep all My commandments,” ’ ” God had exclaimed, “ ‘ “that it might be well with them and their children forever!” ’ ” (Deuteronomy 5:29).

Within that same oration, Moses returned to the “might be well” theme three more times (Deuteronomy 5:32, 33; 6:18; 12:28). The context offered rich blessings: spiritual excellence, material wealth, social harmony, physical vigor, and godly children.

The Hebrew people never did get the “full share” of these blessings. What about Seventh-day Adventists today? Does carelessness about Sabbath preparation and observance also rob us of many blessings?

**Bless and bless**

Jabez's first sentence, in 1 Chronicles 4:11, went like this: "O that you would bless me *indeed*." In *The Prayer of Jabez,* Bruce Wilkinson points out that in Hebrew adding the word "indeed" to the prayer was like "adding five exclamation points, or writing the request in capital letters and underlining it" (22).

The author of 1 Chronicles wrote, "His mother called his name Jabez, saying, 'Because I bore him in pain' " ( 4:9). The birth may have been exceptionally painful, or perhaps she had lost her husband. The future looked dark. With a name like that, the future of Jabez possibly seemed dark, too. Richardson writes of Jabez weighed down "by the sorrow of his past and the dreariness of his present" (ibid.). He sees his prayer as saying, "O 'Father! O Father! Please bless me! And what I really mean is . . . bless me a lot' " (ibid.).

God told Abraham, " 'I will bless you . . . and you shall be a blessing' " (Genesis 12:2). In my Workshop in Prayer class we underline that promise on the first day of our Bible marking of promises. On the board I generally write a paraphrase in which God tells Abraham: " 'I promise that I'll bless you with everything I have—bless and bless and bless!' " (Hebrews 6:14, *The Message*).

I tell the students, "At Calvary God indeed blessed with everything He had, but His blessing doesn't stop there. He blesses and blesses and blesses!"

So it must have been with Jabez. Back to the five-part series about the prayer of Jabez that Dwight Nelson of the University campus church did during the summer of 2000. In the first of the series, Nelson suggested there is a parallel to the *indeed* of Jabez in this promise upon faithful tithe-payers:

> "Bring all the tithes into the storehouse, that there may be food in My house, and try Me now in this," says the Lord of hosts, "If I will not open for you the windows of heaven and pour out for you such blessing that there will not be room enough to receive it" (Malachi 3:10).

A blessing *indeed!* And from Malachi: *A blessing that there will not be room enough to receive it!* Our own faithfulness determines what or how much God can do. Proverbs 3:9, 10 puts it like this: "Honor the Lord with your possessions, and with the firstfruits of all your increase; So your barns will be filled with plenty."

The *firstfruits,* of course, would be the tithe, or 10 percent of the increase (Leviticus 27:30, 32). The context of the above passage from Malachi 3 urges that we not rob God in " 'tithes *and* offerings' " (Malachi 3:8, emphasis supplied). Consider a comment:

> Whenever God's people, in any period of the world, have cheerfully and willingly carried out His plan in systematic benevolence and in gifts

> and offerings, they have realized the standing promise that prosperity should attend all their labors just in proportion as they obeyed His requirements (*Testimonies for the Church,* 3:395).

*Just in proportion!* "When they robbed God in tithes and in offerings they were made to realize that they were not only robbing Him but themselves, for He limited His blessings to them just in proportion as they limited their offerings to Him (ibid.). As you deal with finances, the following promise of Jesus sounds almost extravagant. But God delights to do what the promise offers.

> "Give, and it will be given to you: good measure, pressed down, shaken together, and running over will be put into your bosom. For with the same measure that you use, it will be measured back to you" (Luke 6:38).

**Chocolates—between meals at that!**

Space here permitted a little coverage of just two subjects, Sabbath observance and tithing. A third topic deals with eating and appetite. In 1889 a young man in Battle Creek had trouble with using drinks with alcohol. Ellen White wrote him a letter now found in volume 5 of the *Testimonies,* titled "Dangers of the Young." The letter included this appeal: "Will you not without delay place yourself in right relation to God?" (514). Then came a suggestion any person tempted with beer, flesh food, junk food, or whatever can use:

> Will you not say, "I will give my will to Jesus, and I will do it now," and from this moment be wholly on the Lord's side? Disregard custom and the strong clamoring of appetite and passion. Give Satan no chance to say: "You are a wretched hypocrite."
>
> Close the door so Satan will not thus accuse and dishearten you. Say, "I will believe, I do believe that God is my helper," and you will find that you are triumphant in God (ibid.).

That's encouraging: *You will find that you are triumphant every time!* I call attention to that in my classes like this: First, I read the above, and point out the importance of the word *say.* I suggest, "We know 'expression deepens impression.' It also strengthens determination. Thus the word 'say' gets mentioned, not once, *but twice.*"

Secondly, I review what to say:

- "I will give my will to Jesus, and I will do it now."
- "I will believe, I do believe, that God is my Helper."

Third, I describe a possible situation where the above two sentences might be needed, possibly like this: "You are at a friend's house for Sabbath lunch, and get served a very adequate meal. After a short walk, all return to the living room for a Bible study. The eight of you find seats in a circle, and open your Bibles to the assigned book, Philippians. After prayer for the study, your host starts around a carton of chocolate candies. A few take a chocolate, others by-pass. As the box approaches you, you silently tell yourself, 'I will give my will to Christ, and I do it now.' Then as you take the carton, you add, 'I will believe, I do believe, that God is my Helper.' Without taking a chocolate, you hand the carton to the next person."

**Application**

- Now imagine a tempting situation where the above sentences would help.
- Commit the above two sentences to memory, and use them.

# 21

# Practice Preventative Praying

**"She is your companion and your wife by covenant. But did He not make them one, having a remnant of the Spirit? . . . Therefore take heed to your spirit, and let none deal treacherously with the wife of his youth. 'For the Lord God of Israel says that He hates divorce' " (Malachi 2:14-16).**

God's words about divorce in Malachi 2 are to husbands, but the mention of "Spirit" and "spirit" applies to wives too. The first *Spirit* refers to the Holy Spirit, and the second to a human's spirit or attitude. Malachi 2 sees the Holy Spirit as part of everything good in marriage, including intimacy.

In America, divorce began when the Plymouth Colony granted the first divorce in 1639. In the South, where the Anglican Church had a strong influence, most of early colonies clung to its stand of indissoluble marriage (Robert Plocheck, South Bend *Tribune,* 23 November 2000, D2). By the 1950s, one marriage in four ended in divorce. The 1970s brought no-fault divorce, and by the 1990s half of American marriages ended in divorce.

Divorce and remarriage has become a major issue in our church as well. In Christ's time, two schools of thought existed among the Pharisees. The school of Shammah, who lived a little before Christ, taught that a man could not divorce his wife unless he found her guilty of some action "contrary to the laws of virtue." Hillel, one of his disciples, taught that a man could put away his wife "if she did not cook his food well, or if he found any woman whom he liked better" (*Cruden's Complete Concordance,* under "divorce" entry).

When the Pharisees tried to trap Jesus with a question about Moses and divorce, He said that what Moses had allowed could be traced to hard hearts (Mark 10:5). He referred to the Genesis law that when two become one, that union should not be dissolved. Later the disciples asked and Jesus "gave it to them straight." He said, " 'A man who divorces his wife so he can marry someone else commits adultery against her. And a woman who divorces her husband so she can marry someone else commits adultery' " (Mark 10:11, 12, *The Message*).

**Preventive prayer**

In *The Incredible Power of Prayer* Roger Morneau included a chapter titled "The Tragedy of Crumbling Homes." He spoke of the increase of divorce as "a spiritual plague," stating that it "especially brings misery to innocent children who can't begin to understand why Mother and Dad can no longer get along, and one of them is now moving out" (104).

*No longer get along.* Why does this happen? Can anything prevent it? On prevention, Morneau writes: "Because of the deceptive power of sin a Christian spouse should be willing to do some serious *preventive praying* regardless of how faithful the husband or wife has been to his or her marriage vows" (107).

He then defines that kind of prayer: "Every day it is good to thank God for having blessed a loved one with grace and strength, for having imparted to him or her divine compassionate love" (ibid.). He mentions that the spouse who wants to spend eternity with his or her partner, as well as have him or her in this life, "must secure the stabilizing influence of the Holy Spirit." He speaks of the Spirit as "that great divine power that alone can impart purity of thought, heart, and life" (ibid.).

**Unfaithful husbands**

In that chapter Morneau tells three experiences, all of which involved unfaithfulness on the part of the husband. Two ended in divorce. The first involved a husband who served as a first elder in a large church and had retired. Regarded as a pillar, he had secretly been spending time with a sex magazine and pornographic tapes. They took in a twenty-year-old student so she could attend a Christian college. One evening the wife arrived home from a meeting an hour earlier than expected, and she found her husband in bed with this student.

The second involved a sixty-year-old man who got sexually involved with a seventeen-year-old foster daughter. The third involved a husband who had gotten sexually involved with his secretary, became very critical of his wife, started drinking and smoking, left her, lost his job, and ended up homeless. About that time Morneau's first book on prayer came off the press. After reading it, this man's wife, much impressed with his chapter "Praying for the Ungodly and Wicked," wrote to ask him if he would join her in praying for her husband. He wrote back to assure her that the Holy Spirit would surely minister the graces of redemption as they prayed for her husband.

Morneau also wrote:

> She was particularly impressed by the fact that before I pray for a person who does not serve God, I first ask that the Father will appropriate the merits of Christ's blood to the person in need (108).

In her letter she said, "When I read in your book that we can pray for the Lord to forgive another's sins I was astounded, and began praying for my husband with new faith and hope" (ibid.).

In 1997 the Review published *The Incredible Power of Prayer,* a summary drawn from Morneau's other books on prayer, as a missionary book. If your spouse has left you, and if you can get a copy from the ABC, please read the chapter on crumbling homes. It tells how God worked through that wife's love and faith to restore that home.

**Solving or preventing nonharmony**

For a right focus for those not yet married, and those willing to pray about the divorce problem, or about personal thoughts on divorce, may I suggest two things?

- Secure the book *The Ministry of Healing,* and carefully study the chapter "Builder of the Home." The first half of this chapter offers help to the unmarried. It gives three qualities a girl should look for in a prospective mate, the three qualities a fellow should look for in a possible wife.

Whether married or unmarried, you would do well to find and mark both the section with the qualities, and the section about how to develop a home that becomes a foretaste of heaven.

- Go to my book *More and Still More—A Passion for All God Offers,* and pray about the five suggestions in the chapter entitled "A Passion for Purity in Christ." The following abbreviates:

1. Let all seek to live this statement from Christ's John 17 prayer, " 'For their sakes I sanctify Myself' " (John 17:19). Almost all of us—happily married, single, whatever—encounter moments of ungodly sexual desire. I can look on any person who is a temptation to me as Christ did, and see them as they might become through my prayers, and declare, *"For their sake* I seek the sanctification from God's Word."

2. If we find ourselves being sexually attracted to someone to whom we have no right, we do well to form the habits of seeing that person as clothed with the righteousness of Christ. I can view all women, even a girl in abbreviated shorts, as potentially clothed with the "white garments" of Revelation 3:18.

3. I can take seriously the cautions against wrong thoughts about others given in Proverbs 5, and remain enraptured with my spouse. Ways "enraptured" gets

translated in other versions include: "infatuated" (RSV); "ravished" (Moffatt); and "continually ravished" (AAT). It's unlikely that anyone who cultivates that kind of experience will look with lust at another person.

4. No matter how physically attractive another person seems, look on him or her as a potential temple for the Holy Spirit. In the context of 1 Corinthians 6:19, 20, Paul discusses sexual impurity. The TEV words verse 20, "So use your bodies for God's glory."

5. When tempted, use the following prayer, drawn from *Christ's Object Lessons,* as an enlargement of the publican's request, " ' "God, be merciful to me a sinner!" ' " (Luke 18:13).

Lord, take my heart; for I cannot give it. It is Thy property. Keep it pure, for I cannot keep it for Thee. Save me in spite of myself, my weak, unchristlike self. Mold me, fashion me, raise me into a pure and holy atmosphere, where the rich current of Thy love can flow through my soul (159).

**Application**

- Commit Luke 18:13 and the preceding prayer to memory, and use it as part of your preventive prayers for your marriage, and, changing the "my" to "our," for all the youth of your congregation.
- If married, secure (from a bookstore or your ABC) a book such as Tim and Beverly LaHaye's *The Act of Marriage,* as a help to make sure your partner finds intimacy with you truly the glue God intended.
- If unmarried, and curious about sex and how to wait, secure from the Voice of Prophecy the book-of-the-month titled *SEX—the Myth and the Magic.*
- If a parent of teens, secure from your ABC Loretta Parker Spivey's *Straight Talk,* and use a few sample chapters for worship, or invite your teen to read it on his or her own.

# 22

## Flood Heaven With Thanksgiving

**"The Word became flesh and made his dwelling among us. We have seen his glory . . . full of grace and truth. . . . From the fullness of his grace we have all received one blessing after another" (John 1:14, 16, NIV).**

When James Wilson decided he wanted a well to augment the water supply on his five-acre tract, he hired J. C. Maxwell, a professional well digger. At 100 feet, no water. At 200 feet, no water. But at 212 feet Maxwell struck an artisan well that produced so much water that it soon flooded the yards of the neighbors and fields behind his home.

At first shovelers tried to dig drainage ditches, but the water was coming too fast. Finally a mechanical ditch digger was brought in. The next evening Wilson called for still more help, and county road equipment was sent to dig a large ditch that linked the flow with an irrigation ditch that served the valley.

M. J. Mundorff, district geologist in the ground-water branch of the Geological Survey office in Tacoma, calculated the flow as 1,600 gallons a minute. At that time Seattle Water Department figures showed that the average water consumption in households was about 50 gallons a person per day. With adequate storage facilities, Wilson would have enough water to provide for a city of 40,000 persons.

Compare Wilson's experience with these two promises of Jesus:

> "Whoever drinks of this water will thirst again, but whoever drinks of the water that I shall give him will never thirst. But the water that I shall give him will become in him a fountain of water springing up into everlasting life" (John 4:13, 14).

> Jesus stood and cried out, saying, . . . "He who believes in Me, as the Scripture has said, out of his heart will flow rivers of living water." But this He spoke concerning the Spirit, whom those believing in Him would receive (John 7:37-39).

The expressions—"a fountain of water springing up," and "rivers of living water"—suggest an artisan flow. Shouldn't we seek to become channels that flow with artisan refreshment? "Anything God has done in the past, He is able to duplicate or exceed," writes Wesley L. Duewel in his book *Mighty Prevailing Prayer* (12).

Isn't it time for Pentecost to be repeated? Shouldn't we seek the Lord like we really expected Him to fulfill His promises to send His Spirit with unprecedented power? Isn't it time for the blessings given on the Day of Pentecost to be duplicated and exceeded?

**Blessing after blessing!**

I trust that by the time you finish the last chapter of this book your heart will be overflowing with a kind of artisan-well gratitude—gratitude illustrated by the above experience.

*One blessing after another!* On Thanksgiving Eve of 2000 my wife and I spent a little time reviewing the blessings of the previous twelve months. I started a written list, and after about three dozen, I stopped. We could echo the last four words of this chapter's passage. *One blessing after another!*

Think about the first sentence: *The Word lived for a while among us.* One time I attended the funeral of a teenager killed in a car accident. At the service the one in charge mentioned that the family had buried this young man's great-grandmother two days earlier. "It's hard to understand," he said, "why a young man of fifteen would also die."

He then directed attention to John 11 and to Christ's words to Martha as she grieved the loss of her brother. " 'I am the resurrection and the life,' " Jesus had told Martha. " 'He who believes in Me, though he may die, he shall live' " (John 11:25).

As I drove home I recalled a statement of Jesus that began, " 'If I had not come . . . ' " (John 15:22). I asked myself, "What would life be like if Jesus hadn't come?"

At the time of Christ's birth faith had grown dim even among the Hebrews. Hope had almost vanished. Death was an awful mystery. Most of the secular philosophers of that day apparently believed that "life is like a flake of snow, fallen on the river, for a moment white, then gone forever." Then Jesus came! And because of that, we have reason for faith and hope—and gratitude—even at a funeral!

**Wonder! Wonderful!**

*"The Word became flesh."* Jesus Christ, the co-Creator of hundreds of billions of galaxies, *became flesh!* That fact alone gives reason for deep gratitude and unceasing wonder!

Paul calls it a "mystery"—God "manifested in the flesh" (1 Timothy 3:16). Believers speak of it as "the most marvelous thing that ever took place in earth or heaven—the incarnation of the Son of God." One writer suggests that in contemplating that wonder "we stand baffled before an unfathomable mystery, that the human mind cannot comprehend. The more we reflect upon it, the more amazing does it appear."

In our imagination let's go back and watch it happen.

Time: late 5 B.C. or early 4 B.C.

*Place: possibly a garden.*

Occasion: the three Executives who run the universe are spending the last minutes they will have together for several decades.

What they are about to do has not been an easy decision for any of them. As they stand there, with the Incarnation only minutes away, they silently review the events that have led to this moment—the rebellion of Lucifer, the creation of the earth, the sin of Adam and Eve, the first lamb sacrificed in Eden, the ministries of the prophets, the failures of the Hebrew people, the rise and fall of empires, the emptiness and sorrow in human hearts.

The silence deepens. For Jesus there is loneliness and pain ahead, and much risk. Lucifer will try to destroy Him almost as soon as He is born. Failing that, he will continually attempt to get Jesus to sin.

For the Father, also, the next thirty-three years hold loneliness, and pain, and risk. If Jesus fails in His mission, if He sins, He will eventually become associated with Lucifer. And then what? Will both eventually have to be destroyed? Would the universe itself survive?

And the Holy Spirit? He doesn't fear the attempts Herod will make to destroy the infant Jesus. A single angel can take care of that. But what if Jesus falls into even one sin? What then?

Do they really want to go through with it? Are they risking too much?

They have discussed this before. Though silent, each reaffirms the decision made earlier. The human race *is* worth the risk! If only one person is saved from eternal death it will be worth all the risk, pain, and suffering.

The Father steps over to Christ. His eyes fill with tears as He embraces Him. "Goodbye, Son."

The Holy Spirit clasps the hand of Christ. "I'll be with You every step of the way," He says quietly.

What happened next cannot be described. Scripture only tells that it happened. "The Word became flesh." Perhaps a cloud enveloped the Son. Perhaps there was a flash of light. Within that cloud or flash of light the co-Creator of the galaxies was compressed into a single cell. By the Spirit, that cell was then implanted into Mary's womb.

Eventually, Mary had to share the story of her pregnancy with Joseph. We can understand his doubt of Mary's story. He knew where babies came from. Even the

*National Enquirer,* had there been one in Jerusalem, wouldn't have accepted a story like Mary's.

But then an angel appeared to Joseph in a dream. " 'Joseph, son of David,' " he said, " 'do not be afraid to take to you Mary your wife, for that which is conceived in her is of the Holy Spirit. And she will bring forth a Son, and you shall call His name Jesus, for He will save His people from their sins' " (Matthew 1:20, 21).

*Salvation from sin!* What greater blessing could Heaven give? What greater reason for fervent praise?

**Life purchased with blood**

"In Him was life," John said of Jesus, "and the life was the light of men" (John 1:4). Peter spoke of the cost of that life. "Knowing that you were not redeemed with corruptible things, like silver or gold, from your aimless conduct received by tradition from your fathers, but with the precious blood of Christ" (1 Peter 1:18, 19).

And as Del Delker has sung, "Each drop of blood bought me a million years." That's an eternal reason for gratitude and praise!

One time Dwight Moody commented: "It is life that men want and value most. If a millionaire on a sinking vessel could buy another six months of life, he would give his millions in an instant." Yet how few show the same concern for *eternal* life!

The thought that Jesus *died on a cross* to obtain these privileges for us seems almost unbelievable—and especially when we recall His pre-incarnation position and dignity!*

Ella M. Robinson, a granddaughter of Ellen White, shared this illustration from her grandmother: "Once I heard her say that if it were possible to think of a person in such sad circumstances that he had no earthly thing to be thankful for, still he had the hope of salvation; that was enough to keep him singing from morning till night" (*The Youth's Instructor,* 23 March 1948, 10).

**Application**

- As you start a prayer, sometimes read aloud to God an expression of adoration and praise from a psalm. (Just in the last fifty psalms, you will find expressions of adoration: 103–108; 111–113; 117; 118; 134–136; and 144–150).
- Evaluate this suggestion: "If the loving-kindness of God called forth more thanksgiving and praise, we would have far more power in prayer. We would abound more and more in the love of God and have more bestowed to praise Him for" (*Testimonies for the Church,* 5:317).
- Over a thirty-day period test the assurance that if we praised God more we would love Him more and also "have more bestowed to praise Him for."

* Adapted from Joe Engelkemier, *Whatever It Takes Praying* (Fallbrook, Calif.: Hart Research Center, 1993), 173-178. Used by permission.

# 23

# Make Your Home a Small Group

**" 'These words which I command you today shall be in your heart. You shall teach them diligently to your children' " (Deuteronomy 6:6, 7).**

Picture yourself as a parent with two small children. Visualize Jesus as a supper guest next Thursday evening. After the meal, you move to the living room. He asks, "Do you have any questions?" You discuss several things, and then you tell Him, "Do You have anything You want to tell us?" He replies, "Yes, as a matter of fact, I do."

He takes a Bible from one of your shelves, opens to the book of Deuteronomy, finds chapter 6, and reads, " 'These words which I command you today shall be in your heart. You shall teach them diligently to your children' " (Deut. 6:6, 7). He adds, "I gave this statement to My servant Moses for the parents in My called-out people. For folk today this verse is doubly important."

Then He picks up a copy of *Child Guidance,* and says, "There are a lot of helps in this book for raising your precious children, but tonight I want to urge you to read the section called "The Power of Prayer" again and again. Let Me read a couple of paragraphs. He first turns to page 520, and reads this:

> In every family there should be a fixed time for morning and evening worship. How appropriate it is for parents to gather their children about them before the fast is broken, to thank the heavenly Father for His protection during the night, and to ask Him for His help and guidance and watch care during the day! How fitting, also, when evening comes, for parents and children to gather once more before Him and thank Him for the blessings of the day that is past!

He then turns a couple of pages, and adds, "I don't see anything you have marked here, but let Me say this: This whole book contains a lot of 'how to' suggestions. Here's one about how you can raise these little ones in such a way they will really enjoy your times of family worship:"

" 'Let the father select a portion of Scripture that is interesting and easily understood; a few verses will be sufficient to furnish a lesson which may be studied and practiced through the day. . . . At least a few verses of spirited song may be sung, and the prayer offered should be short and pointed' " (ibid., 522).

"I need to go shortly," your Guest says. "But here's one more important paragraph: 'Let the services be brief and full of life, adapted to the occasion, and varied from time to time. . . . It will add to the interest of the children if they are sometimes permitted to select the reading. Question them upon it, and let them ask questions. Mention anything that will serve to illustrate its meaning' " (ibid.).

As He goes to the door, He picks up your youngest, a three-year-old-girl, hugs her, and kisses her on the forehead. He does the same for your five-year-old son.

**After your Guest leaves**

After Jesus has left, you open *Child Guidance.* In your research you discover:

> In every Christian home God should be honored by the morning and evening sacrifices of prayer and praise. . . . It is the duty of Christian parents, morning and evening, by earnest prayer and persevering faith, to make a hedge about their children (*Counsels to Parents, Teachers, and Students,* 110).

You also discover this about personal prayer:

> When you rise in the morning, kneel at your bedside, and ask God to give you strength to fulfill the duties of the day, and to meet its temptations. . . . Ask Him to help you speak words that will inspire those around you with hope and courage, and draw you nearer to the Saviour (*Sons and Daughters of God,* 199).

In my Workshop in Prayer class, I suggest for families, and for family worship, what I call "Trio Prayer," "Quartet Prayer," "Quintet Prayer," and "Sextet Prayer" groups. Before I explain these to the class, we look at two Bible statements:

- "Likewise the Spirit also helps in our weaknesses. For we do not know what we should pray for as we ought, but the Spirit Himself makes intercession for us with groanings which cannot be uttered" (Romans 8:26).

- "If anyone sins, we have an Advocate with the Father, Jesus Christ the righteous" (1 John 2:1).

I then explain the preceding types of prayer groups—groups especially good for family prayers. I tell them, "If I pray alone, the two divine Beings in these texts join me as I pray, which makes it a trio. When my wife and I pray together upon arising or at bedtime, these two more make it a quartet group. And if another family member joins us, that makes five, a quintet. And so on."

**For the unmarried**

Most of the students are unmarried undergraduates, so I add, "On the firsst night you and your spouse spend together, kneel and pray for each other, and for God's blessing during your first time of intimacy. You will have two divine Beings as prayer Partners. And incidentally, the Holy Spirit of Malachi 2, who blesses as two become 'one' in Christian marriage (Malachi 2:15), will be with you as you continue 'quartet praying.'

"And for continued harmony between you and your spouse, read and follow this command given through Paul, an appropriate word of guidance for newlyweds: 'You should practice tenderhearted mercy and kindness to others. . . . Be gentle and ready to forgive; never hold grudges. Remember, the Lord forgave you, so you must forgive others' (Colossians 3:12, 13, TLB).

"As you live your new lives in Christ, pray for each other again and again, with a prayer like this one: 'I thank God . . . [for you] as without ceasing I remember you in my prayers night and day' (2 Timothy 1:3)."

On that subject consider this suggestion:

> Home should be made all that the word implies. It should be a little heaven upon earth, a place where the affections are cultivated. . . . Our happiness depends upon this cultivation of love, sympathy, and true courtesy to one another" (*Testimonies for the Church*, 3:539).

**Praying with children**

In chapter 12 we explored the wonder of Spirit-filled living—something Jesus had in mind when He said, " 'He who believes in Me, as the Scripture has said, out of his heart shall flow rivers of living water' " (John 7:38). As to the influence from being thus filled, something previously cited:

> The heart that receives the word of God . . . is like the mountain stream fed by unfailing springs, whose cool, sparkling waters leap from rock to rock, refreshing the weary, the thirsty, the heavy laden (*Christ's Object Lessons*, 130).

Think of this: Does not refreshing others, including children, relate to your use of your Bible, and your taking time for family worship? This for parents: "By your own example teach your children to pray with clear, distinct voice. Teach them to lift their heads from the chair and never to cover their faces with their hands. Thus they can offer their simple prayers, repeating the Lord's prayer in concert (*Child Guidance,* 522, 523).

With children, and in any prayer group, ending a season of prayer by repeating the Lord's Prayer "in concert" can bring rich blessings. We do well to vary this from time to time so we stay away from this becoming a meaningless repetition, just a form. One variation can be this: with each of the six requests of the Lord's Prayer, precede each of the six with these words: "Yours is the kingdom, and the power, and the glory, therefore . . ." (see 1 Chronicles 29:11).

For example: "Yours is the kingdom, the power, and the glory, *therefore* hallow Thy name." "Yours is the kingdom, the power, and the gory, *therefore* Thy kingdom come."

*Therefore* can be used with other Bible statements, such as:

- "In Your hand is power and might," *therefore* . . . (1 Chronicles 29:12).
- "Great is our Lord, and mighty in power," *therefore* . . . (Psalm 147:5).
- "His mercy endures forever," *therefore* . . . (Psalm 136:1).
- " 'You are worthy . . . for You were slain, and have redeemed us to God by Your blood,' " *therefore* . . . (Revelation 5:9).
- " 'Salvation and glory and honor and power belong to the Lord our God!' " *therefore* . . . (Revelation 19:1).

**Application**

- What idea in this chapter could bring additional blessing to you as a family? Review the idea about establishment of a new habit (chapter 4), and pray about a new habit you would like to begin.

# 24

## Use Bible Biographies

**"Your words were found, and I ate them" (Jeremiah 15:16).**

Over Thanksgiving of 2000, house guests of my wife and I included nine-year-old Cheryl, a granddaughter. The first morning, at worship, she asked for a story. I read the following from *The Official 1993 Devotional Book,* by Renee Kempf Coffee:

> Edward turned angrily to the lawyer assigned to distribute the property of Edward's recently deceased mother. "Do you mean all Mother left me in her will was her Bible? A Bible! She gave Beth the house! Ginny got the car and the furniture! And all I get is an old book?"
>
> The lawyer shrugged his shoulders. "I'm sorry, Edward. But that's what she put in her will. And when I talked with her last week, she stressed that you got the Bible—and this letter. I'm sure there must be something important about this Bible."
>
> Edward picked up the Bible and letter and stomped from the office. When he got home he opened the envelope, and read the letter. It said: "Dear Son, Please take good care of my Bible. Read its words and you will find a great treasure. Love, Mother."
>
> Picking up the Bible, he shoved it next to a collection of mystery novels in his bookcase. "I'll take care of it, Mother, but I won't read it."
>
> Years passed. Edward's life went from bad to worse. Finally he remembered the Bible his mother had given him. Pulling it out of the bookcase he began reading the story of Jesus. He realized what a mistake it had been to turn his back on God.

As he turned the page, a piece of paper fluttered to the floor. Edward bent over to pick it up. A hundred-dollar bill. How did that get into the Bible? he wondered. Curious, he turned the Bible upside down and shook it. More $100 bills fluttered to the floor. At last Edward understood.

For each of us the Bible contains treasures better than $100 bills. These include:

- friendship with Jesus
- freedom from sin
- eernal life

**More about the biographies**

For parents, nothing equals the Bible stories. The same is true for those who lead prayer meetings. For a resource see especially the chapter in *Education* titled "Bible Biographies." The opening paragraph begins: "As an educator no part of the Bible is of greater value than are its biographies" (146). What themes for family worship! What blessings in these biographies for the midweek service!

For teens and young adults, *Messages to Young People,* in the chapter "Choice of Reading," declares this: "The Bible is our guide to a higher, better life. It contains the most interesting and the most instructive history and biography that were ever written. Those whose imagination has not become perverted by the reading of fiction will find the Bible the most interesting of books" (273, 274).

**An adventure in discovery**

In His Matthew 13 Sermon by the Sea, Jesus told eight stories. In number eight He made this comparison: " 'Therefore every scribe instructed concerning the kingdom of heaven is like a householder who brings out of his treasure things new and old' " (Matthew 13:52). As we interpret this in my Workshop in Prayer class we see the householder as the believer. The treasury? The Bible. The "new" could be two things: (1) new information, and (2) new insights. The "old"? Truths already known, but here, too, one will often discover new insights and/or applications.

I then suggest to my classes: "Every day you should learn something new from the Scriptures" (*My Life Today,* 22). I encourage students to do at least three weeks of journaling, and mention that in my own journaling I try to record a "something new" discovery almost every day. That practice helps keep Bible study refreshing and even exciting.

I mention the awesome benefits:

- The youth who finds his joy in reading the Word of God, and in the hour of prayer, will be constantly refreshed" (*Sons and Daughters of God,* 136).

- The creative energy that called the worlds into existence is in the word of God. . . . It transforms the nature and re-creates the soul in the image of God (*Education,* 126).

**If you like adventure**

Our next objective in this chapter is to explore three methods of Bible study that can increase the interest of the entire family in God's Word.

1. **The "You are there" method.** I suggest this one primarily for private study of a Bible narrative. At a later time family members could share their discoveries. For this method you read a narrative, such as Mark 4:35-41 (Jesus stilling the storm), and ask three questions: "What to see? What to hear? What to feel?" Use your imagination and put yourself into the picture. If you are journaling, write out brief answers to each question. If not, just try to see it the way you would if actually there.

2. **Underlining and using Bible promises.** God's Word contains awesome power (Hebrews 4:12; Isaiah 55:10). As mentioned, for more than ten years my Workshop in Prayer class used *My Life Today* for devotional reading. While going through the January readings, one per day, we underlined this; "If we commit the keeping of our souls to God in the exercise of living faith, his promises will not fail us; for they have no limit but our faith" (14).

3. **Looking for Bible phrases and/or Bible prayers you can study, sometimes memorize, and use as you pray.** Mary's ten-verse prayer recorded in Luke 1:46-55 includes thoughts from no less than eighteen Old Testament passages. Jonah's prayer from the belly of the whale (Jonah 2:2-9) includes several expressions from the Psalms. Nehemiah's prayer in chapter 1 of his book has many similarities to Daniel's prayer in Daniel 9—which suggests that Nehemiah may have had a copy of Daniel's prayer open before him as he prayed. When praying for youth of the world church, I am currently using Joel 2:28-30—about the outpouring of God's Spirit. This paraphrase of a prayer of Paul inspires one to really pray: "Every time I say your name in prayer—which is practically all the time—I thank God for you" (2 Timothy 1:3, *The Message*).

The Bible prayers we memorize in my classes include: Psalm 90:16, 17; Philippians 1:9-11; Psalm 67; and sometimes Ephesians 3:14-19. In *30 Days to a More Powerful Prayer Life* we included a chapter titled "Praying for Adventist Pastors." We built it around the following prayer from Colossians 1:9-14, as cited here:

> We . . . do not cease to pray for you, and to ask that you may be filled with the knowledge of His will in all wisdom and spiritual understanding; that you may have a walk worthy of the Lord, fully pleasing Him, being fruitful in every good work and increasing in the knowledge of God; strengthened with all might, according to His glorious power,

> for all patience and longsuffering with joy; giving thanks to the Father who has qualified us to be partakers of the inheritance of the saints in the light.

The wording of Bible prayers, when merged with trust in the blood of Christ, can add many of the following as you intercede for others:

- Brings an inflow of God's "creative power" into your prayers (Hebrews 4:12).
- Increases your sense of expectation (Romans 10:17).
- Restrains Satan, and even causes him to tremble.
- Gives God the right to act with power (Luke 11:9).

**Application**

- Use the list of three treasures the Bible contains, as listed at the end of the story about Edward, and add others to it.
- If giving a testimony at prayer meeting, which idea from this chapter would you share?

# 25

# Teach From Nature

**"I look up at your macro-skies, dark and enormous, your hand-made sky jewelry, moon and stars mounted in their setting . . . Birds flying and fish swimming, whales singing in the ocean deeps. God, brilliant Lord, your name echoes around the world" (Psalm 8:3-9, *The Message*).**

"When I consider Your heavens, the work of Your fingers, the moon and the stars, which You have ordained, . . . What is man that You are mindful of him, and the son of man that You visit him? For You have made him to have dominion over the works of Your hands; You have put all things under his feet, all sheep and oxen—even the beasts of the field, the birds of the air, and the fish of the sea that pass through the paths of the seas. O Lord, our Lord, how excellent is Your name in all the earth!" (Psalms 8:3, 4, 6-9, NKJV).

It surely is! In a passage about nature as a teacher, Job used expressions such as:

- The beasts will teach you.
- The birds will tell you.
- The earth will teach you.
- The fish will explain to you.

The full passage: " 'But now ask the beasts, and they will teach you; and the birds of the air, they will tell you; Or speak to the earth, and it will teach you; and the fish of the sea will explain to you. Who among all these does not know that the hand of the Lord has done this, in whose hand is the life of every living thing, and the breath of all mankind?' " (Job 12:7-10).

*Teach. Tell. Explain.* Sounds like a classroom, doesn't it? And the book of nature delights children, and much of humanity. An example, a duck named Waddles—a story from *Morning Riser.* I first read it to a granddaughter named Cheryl. Over the following two years she had me read it to her at least five more times.

**A duck named Waddles**

Susie, a two-year-old, got a baby duck as a gift for her birthday. Waddles stayed close to Susie as she built sandcastles in her sandbox.

When baby Carol was born two years later, Waddles, now a large, strong duck, realized he had a new responsibility. Settling down by her cradle with a wild cry, he became her guard. Whenever the baby was taken to the backyard for a sunbath, Waddles waited with great excitement. His place? Beneath the baby's buggy, watching constantly.

The busy mother appreciated Waddles, for Susie and her friends sometimes forgot to close the back gate. But nothing, man or beast, could enter that gate with Waddles around.

One morning, while Waddles watched the baby from his spot under the buggy, the mother got a telephone message, "I just saw a mad dog go into your driveway."

"Did the children leave the gate open?" the mother wondered. Before she could run to the yard, she heard a high, wild honk. The dog had entered the yard! As she rushed through the back door, she saw the dog. That rabid animal had stopped just feet from the baby—Waddles flying at him, his beak snapping. Grabbing the baby, the mother ran into the house and slammed the door.

Quickly she called the police, then waited as she listened to the battle-mixture of growls, barks, and flapping wings. If only Waddles would fly out of danger. But the brave duck wanted to be sure the dog did not hurt his helpless little friend. When the police arrived, the dog lay dead, just outside the gate. Waddles's lifeless body blocked the gate.

The authors, Eileen and Jay Lantry, drew this parallel: "Jesus, too, never stopped in His terrible struggle with the enemy until He gained the victory. But it cost His life that we, His friends, might live" (110).

**Nature for parents, teachers, pastors**

The chapter that follows, "Use Lots of Stories," relates that Christ drew many of His illustrations from the book of nature. Several paragraphs in the *Christ's Object Lessons* introductory chapter, "Teaching in Parables," deal with this. That chapter speaks of Christ's love for the things of nature. "He might have made suggestions in scientific lines that would have afforded food for thought and stimulus for invention to the close of time. But He did not do this" (22, 23).

Instead, Jesus taught people to behold God as shown in His works, His Word, and by His providences. "He spoke to men of those truths that relate to the conduct of life, and that take hold upon eternity" (ibid., 23).

Another book, *Counsels to Parents, Teachers, and Students*—and pastors also—declares: "There is a simplicity and purity in these lessons direct from nature that makes them of the highest value to others besides the heathen. The children and youth, all classes of students, need the lessons to be derived from this source" (186).

The same source mentions this: "In itself the beauty of nature leads the soul away from sin and worldly attractions, and toward purity, peace, and God" (ibid.).

**Very human—yet more than human**

Jesus had a favorite title for Himself—"the Son of Man." He used it nearly sixty times in the Gospels. I love that fact about Christ! As a Man, He wants to be a trusted Companion to every man. He seeks to impart courage—and beauty—to every woman. He desires the devotion of every teenager. He seeks the love of every child.

He was and is more than just a Man, however. The Bible presents Him as the co-Creator of all the hundreds of billions of galaxies in known space. John wrote, "All things were made through Him, without Him nothing was made that was made" (John 1:3).

His "goings forth," wrote Micah, had been "from of old, from everlasting" (5:2, KJV). He knows the name of each star and galaxy—He "brings out the starry host" and "calls them each by name" (Isaiah 40:26, NIV). Before becoming a man He had traveled "from star to star, from world to world, superintending all, by His providence supplying the needs of every order of being in His vast creation" (*Patriarchs and Prophets,* 69).

And a "vast creation" it is!

**His galactic empire**

"Lift your eyes and look to the heavens," God invites (Isaiah 40:26, NIV). With the naked eye we see about 3,000 stars in each hemisphere. Most are comparatively close neighbors.

We also see the merged light of billions of stars within the Milky Way. The stars—suns—in this "river of light" appear to touch each other, but a telescope reveals that vast distances separate them. The average distance between stars is about six light-years.

(A light-year is the distance that light travels in a year—at 11 million miles a minute, 16 billion miles every 24 hours, 6 trillion miles in a year!) Our Galaxy contains at least 100 billion suns. Few can grasp how much it takes to make even one billion. For example:

- There have been only a little over one billion minutes since the birth of Christ.
- If you had inherited a billion dollars at the time of Christ, and had spent $1,000 a day ever since, you would still have enough money left to keep on spending $1,000 a day for another 750 years!

The billions of suns in our Galaxy are arranged in the shape of a huge spiral. Our sun is located about three-fifths way out from the center. When we look out from the plane of this disk-like spiral, we see individual stars. When we look toward the center of the spiral, as we do in the summer in this hemisphere, we get a milky effect from the merged light of millions of suns.

**God's greatness and splendor**

Most astronomy books suggest that our Galaxy is about 100,000 light-years across and about 2,000 light years thick. Imagine crossing it from rim to rim in a Boeing 747! At 600 miles an hour it would take 115 billion years to cross!*

There are hundreds of billions of galaxies within known space. The next time you look at the Big Dipper, consider this: if you could see the bowl of that Dipper the way a large telescope views and photographs it, you would find a million galaxies just in the bowl!*

David wrote, "The heavens declare the glory of God" (Psalm 19:1). As telescopes probe deeper and deeper into space, we can only exclaim, " 'Yours, O Lord, is the greatness, the power and the glory, the victory and the majesty' " (1 Chronicles 29:11).

**Application**

- If your family includes small children, or grandchildren, read them the story of Waddles; they'll enjoy it too.

* Adapted from Joe Engelkemier, *Whatever It Takes Praying* (Fallbrook, Calif.: Hart Research Center, 1993), 37, 38. Used by permission.

# 26

## Use Lots of Stories

**" 'I will open My mouth in parables; I will utter things kept secret from the foundation of the world' " (Matthew 13:35).**

Jesus liked to use stories. Matthew 13, with eight parables, shows that. Matthew quoted the above from a Messianic prophecy found in Psalm 78:2. Jesus used a lot of illustrations from nature, and others from daily life, as with a house built on sand. In the Sermon on the Mount one can count some two dozen illustrations. He drew lessons from news events as well, like in Luke 13:1-5, where He drew truth from a tower that fell and killed some people and from the murder of some Galileans by Pilate.

The Spirit of Prophecy also contains a lot of illustrations. A sample includes a hawk pursuing a dove (*My Life Today,* 105), untrained horses (ibid., 39), a field left uncultivated (ibid., 83), moth-eaten clothing (ibid., 269). This illustration from *Testimonies for the Church* I don't think any parent could ever forget:

> If one of your children were in the river, battling with the waves and in imminent danger of drowning, what a stir there would be! What efforts would be made, what prayers would be offered, what enthusiasm manifested, to save the human life! But here are your children out of Christ, their souls unsaved. . . . They are perishing without hope and without God in the world, and you are careless and unconcerned (5:424).

The book *Education* makes this suggestion:

> The teacher [parent, pastor, elder] should constantly aim at simplicity and effectiveness. He should teach largely by illustration, and even in deal-

> ing with older pupils [adult listeners] should be careful to make every explanation plain and clear (233).

*He should teach largely by illustration.* Saving illustrations does not take an expensive file. I own some file cabinets, in which I keep 8½-by-11-inch manila folders, alphabetically arranged. But I keep an overflow of illustrations in an ordinary cardboard box, such as you can get at a grocery store, from their discards.

**The Scars**

When you read or hear an attention-getting illustration, try to get a copy. For example, for the mission story last Sabbath (12/10/00) a teenager named Tiffany used a story from the Internet titled "The Scars." I will never forget it; I don't think you will either: On a hot day in south Florida a little boy—we will call him Jerry—decided to go for a swim in the lake behind his house. In a hurry to dive into the cool water, he ran out the back door, leaving his shoes, socks, and shirt as he ran. He flew into the water. As he swam toward the middle of the lake, an alligator headed toward the shore Jerry had just left. His mother—from the house—saw the two as they got closer and closer together. As she ran toward the water, she yelled as loud as she could. Jerry, as he heard her voice, became alarmed, and made a U-turn to swim toward his mother. But it was too late. Just as he reached her at the shore, the alligator reached him.

Jerry's mother grabbed him just as the alligator seized his legs. That began a fierce tug-of-war between the two. The stronger-than-the-mother alligator battled for Jerry, but the mother would not release her grip on his arms. A farmer happened to drive by, heard the screams, raced from his truck, took aim with a gun, and shot the alligator.

Jerry spent weeks in the hospital—his legs terribly scarred by the hungry alligator. And on his arms, his mother's fingernails dug into Jerry's flesh in her effort to hang on to her son. A newspaper reporter interviewed Jerry some time later, and asked if he would show the scars. Jerry lifted his pant legs. And then with obvious pride, he said to the reporter: "But look at my arms. I have big scars on my arms, too. I have them because my mom would not let go."

You and I can identify with Jerry. We too possess scars. No, not from an alligator, but the scars from a sinful past. Some of those scars have caused deep regret. But some wounds are because Jesus would not let go. In the midst of your struggle with sin, He has been there holding on to you.

If you choose Jesus as your Savior, you are a child of God. He wants to protect you and provide for you in every way. But sometimes we wade into dangerous situations. The swimming hole of life has many dangers—and we tend to forget the enemy lurks close by to attack and devour. That's when the tug-of-war begins. If you have the scars of His love on your arms be very, very grateful. He did not—and will not—let you go.

**Application**

- Share the above story with a child or grandchild.

# 27

# Exhibit Clarity and Enthusiasm

**"So they read distinctly from the book . . . and they gave the sense, and helped them to understand the reading" (Nehemiah 8:8).**

Paul once wrote, "Unless you utter by the tongue words easy to understand, how will it be known what is spoken? For you will be speaking into the air" (1 Corinthians 14:9). Now a paraphrase: *Unless you pray with a clear, distinct voice, how will anyone be blessed by hearing you pray?*

During family worship, or saying grace, or at a prayer group, can *just hearing you pray* touch the hearers? "Fervent and effectual prayer is always in place, and will never weary. Such prayer interests and refreshes all who have a love for devotion" (*Testimonies for the Church,* 2:582).

In order to refresh listeners, does it not also need to be clear and distinct? May I ask two questions?

- In a month's time how often on the average do you hear someone pray so softly that you get very few of his or her words?
- Do you ever attend a prayer group where one of the pray-ers puts their head down on the bench or chair, and prays so timidly that no one understands the words?

To help bring improvement, what help do you see in the opening verse? Could that also be paraphrased? Perhaps to say: *So they prayed distinctly, and blessed many in the same group.*

Before we look at how enthusiasm can bless others even as you pray, a few words about distinctness. "Let those who pray and those who speak pronounce their words properly and speak in clear, distinct, even tones. . . . Satan rejoices when the prayers offered to God are almost inaudible. . . . Let the testimonies borne and the prayers offered be clear and distinct (*Testimonies,* 6:382).

**The contagiousness of enthusiasm**

The citation about teaching largely by illustration comes from a chapter in *Education* titled "Methods of Teaching." The paragraph following that one talks about enthusiasm:

> An important element in educational work is enthusiasm. On this point there is a useful suggestion in a remark once made by a celebrated actor. The archbishop of Canterbury had put to him the question why actors in a play affect their audiences so powerfully by speaking of things imaginary, while ministers of the gospel often affect theirs so little by speaking of things real (233).

" 'With due submission to your grace,' replied the actor, 'permit me to say that the reason is plain: It lies in the power of enthusiasm. We on the stage speak of things imaginary as if they were real, and you in the pulpit speak of things real as if they were imaginary' " (ibid.). "The teacher in his work," the next paragraph points out, "is dealing with things real, and he should speak of them with all the force and enthusiasm which a knowledge of their reality and importance can inspire" (ibid.).

Could the above lack of enthusiasm be one reason pastors or elders do not get more people out for mid-week services? Does that explain why as parents we at times find our children bored with family worship? Sports events often awaken enthusiasm. But consider this: *enthusiasm* comes from two Greek words, *en* (in) and *theos* (God). That kind of enthusiasm lasts. But as for sports, a tennis star once said, "The thrill of winning lasts about an hour."

Consider this comment about the contagious power of enthusiasm as illustrated by Nehemiah: Through Nehemiah's prayers, enthusiasm, and influence, an unfinished task that had lingered for more than sixty years was completed *in fifty-two days!*

About 450 B.C., the people in Jerusalem probably thought that they would never again enjoy security. Some sixty years earlier, the returned exiles had rebuilt the temple. The walls of Jerusalem had been partly reconstructed also. But nothing much had been done.

Then around 450 B.C, enemies destroyed most of the rebuilt sections. If you had lived then, you would have had every reason to be frightened. Wild beasts roamed the woods and fields. Bands of robbers wandered through the countryside to plunder and kill. The wall about a town or city often meant the difference between a night of peaceful sleep and a night filled with fear.

To the residents of Jerusalem it must have seemed they would always be living in fear.

Nehemiah learned about these new dangers while serving at the palace of King Artaxerxes at Susa. About December of the twentieth year of Artaxerxes's reign, Nehemiah's brother Hanani and other visitors from Judah came to the Persian capital. " 'Those who survived the exile and are back in the province are in great trouble and disgrace,' " they told Nehemiah. " 'The wall of Jerusalem is broken down, and its gates have been burned with fire' " (Nehemiah 1:3, NIV).

When he heard this, Nehemiah sat down and wept. "For some days," he said, "I mourned and fasted and prayed before the God of heaven" (Nehemiah 1:4, NIV). The next seven verses record his prayer—a petition that makes a good pattern when you need to ask God to do something. Note these four parts:

1. **Adoration.** He addresses his Creator as a " 'great and awesome God' " (v. 5, NIV).
2. **Confession.** Nehemiah confesses his sins, and the sins of his people (vs. 6, 7).
3. **Confidence.** He cites promises from the book of Deuteronomy with confidence they will be fulfilled (vs. 8-10).
4. **Commitment.** He is willing to be used by God to help bring an answer to his own prayer (v. 11).

**A plan**

While Nehemiah prayed, a plan came to mind. As cupbearer for Artaxerxes, he would speak to the king about the situation in Jerusalem. He ended his prayer with this plea: " 'O Lord, let your ear be attentive to the prayer of this your servant. . . . Give your servant success today by granting him favor in the presence of this man' " (Nehemiah 1:11, NIV).

An opportunity did not come that day, however. Nor the next. Nor the next. But Nehemiah kept praying. As he prayed his faith and courage increased. The author of *Prophets and Kings* summarizes the spirit of his prayers:

> His mouth was filled with holy arguments. He pointed to the dishonor that would be cast upon God, if His people, now that they had returned to Him, should be left in weakness and oppression (629).

Nehemiah backed his "arguments" with Scripture cited from Deuteronomy 4:29-31. God had warned that sin could cause His people to be scattered to the ends of the earth. But He also promised that upon repentance He would restore them to their homes. Nehemiah was confident the Lord would fulfill that promise.

Nehemiah's "arguing with God" and his claiming of promises continued for four months. And the longer he prayed, the stronger his concern became. That concern eventually helped to open a door of opportunity. Nehemiah spent so much time in confession of sin and in earnest pleading that it began to tell on his health.

One day that spring, as he took the king's wine to him, Artaxerxes eyed him suspiciously. " 'Why does your face look so sad when you are not ill?' " the king asked. " 'This can be nothing but sadness of heart' " (Nehemiah 2:2, NIV).

That frightened Nehemiah. He feared Artaxerxes would think him part of a plot to overthrow him. Nehemiah explained the cause for his concern, and the king asked, "What is it that you want?"

Before he replied, Nehemiah darted a silent prayer to heaven. "I prayed to the God of heaven," he said (Nehemiah 2:4, NIV). That quick prayer won to his side a power that could turn the heart of even a heathen king. And Nehemiah didn't just ask for permission to go. He also requested a safe-conduct and supplies. "Because the gracious hand of my God was upon me," Nehemiah reported, "the king granted my requests" (Nehemiah 2:8, NIV).

**Much prayer**

When Nehemiah arrived in Jerusalem, he found a discouraged people. The third night there, he took a few trusted men and surveyed the broken-down walls and the burned gates. "The officials did not know where I had gone or what I was doing," he later wrote, "because as yet I had said nothing to the Jews or the priests or nobles or officials" (Nehemiah 2:16, NIV).

He spent the rest of the night in prayer. He knew that he would need the power of God the next morning as he tried to rouse his dispirited countrymen. God spoke through him. " 'Come, let us rebuild the wall of Jerusalem,' " he urged (Nehemiah 2:17, NIV). He reinforced his request with a faith-building testimony: "I also told them about the gracious hand of my God upon me and what the king had said to me" (Nehemiah 2:18, NIV).

That brought a positive response! " 'Let us start rebuilding,' " the people said (Nehemiah 2:18, NIV). With a "whatever it takes" spirit, Nehemiah threw everything he had into the work. This summarizes his influence:

> His holy purpose, his high hope, his cheerful consecration to the work, were contagious. The people caught the enthusiasm of their leader, and in his sphere each man became a Nehemiah (Ellen White, *The SDA Bible Commentary,* 3:1137).

Nehemiah kept in close touch with the workers. He spoke courage to the fearful, and words of approval to the diligent. He prayed fervently and constantly. " 'The God of heaven,' " he exclaimed again and again, " 'will give us success' " (Nehemiah 2:20, NIV).

As Nehemiah chapter 5 and 6 show, many problems arose, but Nehemiah met every problem with prayer combined with a "whatever it takes" spirit. Near the end of chapter 6, Nehemiah gives this report: "So the wall was completed on the twenty-fifth of Elul [August-September], in fifty-two days" (v. 15, NIV).

*Fifty-two days!**

**"We need Nehemiahs"**

Do you see a parallel for this first decade of the new millennium? Revelation 14 introduces an angel flying through the heavens with what John called "the everlasting gospel"—a gospel to be taken "to every nation, tribe, tongue, and people" (Revelation 14:6).

This angel is followed by two more—each with a distinctive end-time message. All are obviously symbolic, for the work assigned to them is that of preaching the everlasting gospel. That preaching has not been entrusted to literal angels; it has been committed to humans. Each of these angels, therefore, symbolizes those who are commissioned to make known to the world the gospel *and* the special truths that constitute the burden of each angel's message.

Revelation 14:12 describes the kind of people the messages of Revelation 14:6-11 produce: "Here is the patience of the saints; here are those who keep the commandments of God and the faith of Jesus." The last seven verses of Revelation 14 then describe the second coming of Jesus. So these messages are to be given to the world *just before Christ returns.* And they are to go to every nation, to every island, to every people group.

In a world were the population increases by more than 70 million people every 12 months, that's a task far more challenging than rebuilding some stone walls!

But with God nothing is impossible. God is well able "to do immeasurably more than all we ask or imagine" (Ephesians 3:20, NIV). Why, then, are there still vast multitudes of people who know nothing of the special truths of Revelation 14?

The Laodician message of Revelation 3 pinpoints a key reason: lukewarmness. " 'I know your works,' " says the True Witness, " 'that you are neither cold nor hot' " (v. 15).

What's the solution?

We need Nehemiahs!

At the start of the Jerusalem project, there was only one Nehemiah. But one became several. Several became dozens. Dozens became hundreds and possibly thousands.

Could that be the challenge for the rest of this decade?

Whatever your position—a young person still in school, lay person, church officer, pastor, church administrator, worker in supporting ministries—could you exert a Nehemiah-like influence as we continue through the new millenium?

Note again these words about Nehemiah: "His holy purpose, his high hope, his cheerful consecration to the work, were contagious. The people caught the enthusiasm of their leader, and in his sphere each man became a Nehemiah."

**Applications**

- Note the four parts in Nehemiah's chapter 1 prayer.
- Try including those four parts as you pray for the Holy Spirit in your life, or on your local congregation.
- Limit any public prayer to one or two minutes, but for private prayer, what might we learn from the book of Nehemiah?
- What do you see as the balance between prayer for the latter rain and enthusiastic leadership?

* Adapted from Joe Engelkemier, *Whatever It Takes Praying* (Fallbrook, Calif.: Hart Research Center, 1993), 21-30. Used by permission.

# 28

# Encourage Prayer Groups

**" 'You shall receive power when the Holy Spirit has come upon you; and you shall be witnesses to Me . . . to the end of the earth' " (Acts 1:8).**

Do you ever pause to think about the fact that our God loves to get attention by doing some pretty striking things? " 'I am going to do something in your days that you would not believe,' " He once said, " 'even if you were told' " (Habakkuk 1:5, NIV).

The above text comes from about 630 B.C. God said that to the prophet Habakkuk in description of dangers from Babylon. Could it describe some of the events now facing us?

If you didn't get to the chapter "The Final Crisis," mentioned in chapter 2, let me urge again that you read it. Consider also this paraphrase of Christ's words about prayer groups: " 'When two of you get together on anything at all on earth and make a prayer of it, my Father in heaven goes into action' " (Matthew 18:19, *The Message*).

What ideas in the following could be turned into prayer requests?

> The time has come for a thorough reformation to take place. When this reformation begins, the spirit of prayer will actuate every believer and will banish from the church the spirit of discord and strife. Those who have not been living in Christian fellowship will draw close to one another. One member working in right lines will lead other members to unite with him in making intercession for the revelation of the Holy Spirit (*Testimonies for the Church,* 8:250, 251)

Does God hope you will become that "one member"? As a "how to," this follows the above:

> The Lord will co-operate with His servants. All will pray understandingly the prayer that Christ taught His servants: "Thy kingdom come. Thy will be done in earth, as it is in heaven." Matthew 6:10 (ibid.).

Notice that two requests come from the Lord's Prayer. The first chapter of *Great Prayers and Pray-ers of the Bible* focuses on how we can use the requests of the Lord's Prayer. Here I want to mention additional possibilities. I love to use the above two requests, along with the first request about hallowing God's name, as I pray for surrendered and Spirit-filled youth and others. I use these requests, in fact, almost every time I pray for children and youth. (More about youth back in chapter 18). Here's what I ask almost every time:

"Father I know You want all the youth in Christian schools. So do I. But what a job You have! I thank You that it's Your plan to grant us, when we pray, what You otherwise would not give. So here's what I ask: that Your name be hallowed in all of them, that Your kingdom now come within to each, and that Your will be done in their lives. Help me to want *all* just as strongly as You do."

**Why God has a hard time**

We do two things that make it difficult for God, who longs for every believer to fully reflect Jesus.

- We pray so little, and so listlessly.
- We bring so much of the world and its entertainment into our homes and schools.

Let me illustrate the matter of entertainment with a prayer of an undergraduate student, as she attempted to get a weekly prayer group started: "I am heartbroken that we are being asked to be like Hollywood instead of like Jesus."

She included the above sentence in a Friday morning prayer that preceded a widely publicized Halloween barn party. In a color advertisement students had been advised: "Dress like a star." The context suggested a Hollywood star.

Do you see why we, even in a Christian environment, make God's job more difficult? We try to be more and more like the world. We ignore words such as these:

> Do not love the world or the things in the world. If anyone loves the world, the love of the Father is not in him. For all that is in the world—the lust of the flesh, the lust of the eyes, and the pride of life—is not of the Father but is of the world (1 John 2:15, 16).

The next sentence declares: "And the world is passing away, and the lust of it; but he who does the will of God abides forever" (v. 17). *The Message* paraphrase puts that warning like this: "Love of the world squeezes out love for the Father." It adds that the world "is on the way out—but whoever does what God wants is set for eternity."

**Praying for revival**

The word *revival* means to renew, to revitalize, to rekindle, to activate, to awaken. Before reading further, ask yourself, "What most needs renewing, rekindling, or reviving in *my* life?"

As you ask and pray, consider these needs:

- a revival of Bible study

At a very low point in Judah's history, Jeremiah wrote a powerful statement about a joy based on God's Word. "Your words were found," he wrote, "and I ate them, and Your word was to me the joy and rejoicing of my heart" (Jeremiah 15:16). And in words through Isaiah God declared, " 'My word . . . shall not return to Me void, but it shall accomplish what I please' " (Isaiah 55:11). Of that time the book *Evangelism* anticipates:

> A revival in Bible study is needed throughout the world. . . . A knowledge of God is the highest education, and it will cover the earth with its wonderful truth as the waters cover the sea (*Evangelism,* 456).

- a revival of personal and family prayer

Does the description of prayer among Seventh-day Adventists as published in the *Review and Herald* in December of 1892 (and cited in chapter 4) ever apply to your family? How about these words?

No time! No time! No time!

Compare that lack of time with these repeated sentences from chapter 4: "These have no time to offer prayer for divine help and guidance, and for the abiding presence of Jesus in the household. They go forth to labor as the horse or ox goes, without one thought of God or heaven. . . . They have little more appreciation of His goodness than have the beasts that perish."

Scripture contains no indication that beasts will be translated. What about human beings—parents, teens, children—who live like "the beasts that perish"?

In my research about what to pray for at home rather than at the church, consider this:

> We should not come to the house of God to pray for our families unless deep feeling shall lead us while the Spirit of God is convicting them. Generally, the proper place to pray for our families is at the family altar (*Testimonies,* 1:145, 146).

It would be good to read the context for the preceding suggestion.

• a revival of congregational/group prayer

Notice in particular the group prayer that took place in the early church: "They all continued with one accord in prayer and supplication" (Acts 1:14). Compare the prayers then with our need now, as cited from the December, 2000 *Signs of the Times*®, where Update reported this:

> George Barna, an evangelical who studies cultural trends, says that in the comparisons his group has made between Christians and non-Christians on more than seventy moral behaviors, they rarely find substantial differences. Christian adults spend seven times more hours each week watching TV than in spiritual pursuits like Bible reading and worship. They spend more time surfing the Internet than they do conversing with God in prayer (7).

The angels especially long to see true revival change that, with a key concern for children. They long to do more and still more for the children. Give thanks for those heavenly beings, and for truths such as the following: "Angels of God are ever near your little ones"(*That I May Know Him,* 42).

As you work with the angels, remember this: "Teach them [your children], when temptations urge into paths of selfish indulgence, . . . to look to Jesus, pleading, 'Save, Lord, that I be not overcome.' Angels will gather about them in answer to their prayers, and lead them into safe paths" (*Fundamentals of Christian Education,* 153).

**Youth prayer groups**

Do teens and young adults possess what it takes to lead out in seeking a greater measure of the Holy Spirit, and in evangelism projects? According to *Summons to the Witness Stand,* the youth Sabbath School quarterly for July-September of 2000, there are places such as parts of Africa and South America where "young people are establishing churches." The quarterly states, "Young adults are the pastors, the elders, and the deaconesses." It adds that in islands in the South Pacific "80 percent of the church membership" consists of people under 30 (24).

But how about those still in their teens? Let me tell you about some from Great Lakes Academy. During the 1997-98 school year, as I ate lunch at the Andrews University cafeteria (my wife works there), students at my table included three first-year students—Debi, Heidi, and Rachel. All through the previous school year they and others had met five days a week at 6:15 A.M. to pray for the Holy Spirit. Debi, an Andrews freshman who had graduated the previous year from that school, led out in organizing that group. "Debi," I asked, "Why this ongoing focus on praying for the Holy Spirit?"

"Because," she replied, "everything that's good comes through the work of the Holy Spirit. I'm beginning to understand that having the Holy Spirit in us is the only way to be like Christ."

"How did you get started?" I asked.

"It was during the 1992-93 school year at Great Lakes Academy. Pastor Pete Neri suggested that students might want to start groups to pray for the Holy Spirit. Students themselves led out in getting groups started. These groups kept growing, and during the 1994-95 school year those in the girls' dorm started meeting together once a week in the front lobby. We often filled the lobby."

**The Spirit as a Helper**

I asked, "Are the three of you finding that praying for the Holy Spirit makes a difference as you live a highly pressured university lifestyle?"

Debi, a nursing major, and Heidi, a religion major, shared experiences in which they had taken extra time for fellowship and prayer that could have been used to hit the books. They told how God had blessed them with better-than-usual recall during quizzes and tests.

Rachael, a junior English/history major, said, "I love praying with others. As others share what God has done for them it inspires me to tell what He has been doing for me. I've had experiences where God has led me when I've had important decisions to make. As I have prayed God has guided me in making right choices."

Debi said, "I work with magabooks, and go out some evenings to sell. I like to pray with people, and the other evening I was not getting a chance to pray with anyone. So I stopped and told the Lord, 'I don't care if I don't sell a single book. I just want a chance to pray with people.' "

"Shortly after that," she continued, "I came to a home where a very poor lady wanted *The Desire of Ages, The Great Controversy,* and *Bible Readings.* She got all the change she had and gave it to me, and I left the books. She let me pray with her. Before the evening was over I had prayed with three different families. I know it was the Holy Spirit."

Debi then added, "And do you know what? God blessed me with $119 in sales that evening! When we pray, and put Him first, He provides for our needs."

Debi and Heidi told of jogging together, and praying as they run. Debi said, "Prayer and God's Spirit, that's the only way, in school, in studies, in friendships, in everything!"

**Application**

- Which of the three areas of revival this chapter suggested could you be the most help in bringing about?
- Could you begin a prayer group of several people, with weekly or bi-weekly meetings at your home?

# 29

## Seek More and More of God's Spirit

**"Be filled with the Spirit, speaking to one another in psalms and hymns and spiritual songs, singing and making melody in your heart to the Lord, giving thanks always for all things to God the Father in the name of our Lord Jesus Christ" (Ephesians 5:18-20).**

As a young mother, Penny Estes Wheeler, now a magazine editor at the Review and Herald, published a viewpoint titled "I Didn't Want the Holy Spirit." She didn't mean speaking in tongues. "I mean that even though I am a follower of Christ, I didn't want the Holy Spirit—period."

She had heard sermons abut being Spirit-filled, and had visions of "an unseen force" compelling her to go to a shopping center, get up by the potted plants, wave her Bible, and threaten those who didn't respond. She sometimes felt guilty. "Still, as a housewife mother, I was too busy, I told myself, to devote days to giving out of religious literature. No. Emphatically, I didn't want the Holy Spirit. I simply didn't have time (*These Times,* October 1976, 22).

Ever feel like Penny, ladies? And, men, does the idea of being Spirit-filled trouble you? If you are a young person, how about you?

### What changed Penny's thinking

Penny said that since childhood she had known about the statement in Galatians 5 concerning the fruits of the Spirit—love, joy, peace. "And then it hit me," she said. Those were the very things people everywhere wanted, yet generally sought in vain. "So," she wrote, "I backed up and started over, interested in just what the Spirit's role should be for me."

Early one morning she started with a study of John 14 –16. Christ had told the disciples He was about to leave. Penny paraphrased what He said like this: "But it is for your benefit that I go, for the Holy Spirit—the Comforter—cannot come until I am gone. When I took a human body, I limited Myself. If I am with you, Peter, in Jerusalem, I can't help you, John, in Samaria."

"I will pray the Father," Jesus continued, "and He shall give you another Comforter, that He may abide with you forever, even the Spirit of truth, for He dwells with you and shall be in you."

Penny then told what happened the February morning she was making new discoveries:

A gray mist hung over the trees as she looked out. She prayed, "Please, Father, let the Holy Spirit live in me all day long. . . . "

A piercing wail filled the house. The baby was awake and hungry. If Penny got to her in time, maybe she wouldn't awaken the other two little ones. "Thank You," God, she prayed as she headed for the bedroom. The baby's cries were replaced with a smile as Penny entered the room and picked her up. Penny wrapped the baby in a blanket, took her to the rocker in the living room, and began to nurse her. "Jesus loves you, little dear," she sang. "We're so glad He is here."

The older girls woke up, cold and cranky, but Penny fixed hot-water bottles and hot cereal. By the time she put the baby in a swing, the girls were ready for a story.

All through the morning, Penny tried to keep sensing the Holy Spirit's presence. A surprising sense of His peace surrounded her. After lunch, as the children began their naps, Penny returned to her Bible. She opened it to John 16. As she read, she concluded the Holy Spirit's presence did not mean fewer troubles. Rather, He helped her have patience when stress arose. Even when He reproved, He was both a Friend and a Comforter.

**A reader responds**

The following came (1999) from a retired librarian who lives in Collegedale, Tennessee. "For prayer meeting the church used your book *More and Still More*, so each person was given a copy. The reason for this letter is the very special chapter on the Holy Spirit, 'A Passion to Become Spirit-filled.' It has given me a whole new outlook in my thinking of the Holy Spirit."

She and her husband had spent the winter of 1998-99 at Avon Park, Florida. She said she had read the book "again and again." She loved my mention of the Holy Spirit "as a very close friend" (44). "This is very special," she added.

It is my prayer that all who read this follow-up book will more and more think of the Holy Spirit "as a very close friend." Are you comfortable with thinking of the Holy Spirit as a person? With added perspective, here are the three suggestions that the writer from Collegedale found helpful:

- Think of the Holy Spirit both as a person and as a very special friend.

In the Bible the Holy Spirit has numerous titles that indicate personality. He has emotions and performs actions that only a personal being could carry out. The Holy Spirit is as loving as Christ Himself. If your eyes could be opened, you could see Him ready to walk through your front door to be with you in your home. If He is welcomed, the benefits are awesome. "The sweetest type of heaven is a home where the Spirit of the Lord presides" (*The Adventist Home,* 15).

• Open your heart totally and completely to the Holy Spirit.

Ask the Holy Spirit, as a precious Friend, to give you the mind of Christ (Philippians 2:5). Invite Him to help you love the things that Christ loves, and to hate the things that He hates. Invite Him to totally possess you—to guide your thoughts, your words, and your actions.

In *Mighty Prevailing Prayer* Wesley Duewel closes his book with a suggested prayer. The following is a paragraph, slightly adapted, that I like to pray in moments of temptation:

> I give myself to You anew. Take me! Take all of me! Take me and fill me with Your Spirit that it may not be I but You living in me, not my love but Your love pouring through me, not my power but Your mighty power working in and through me. Fill me so that it may not be I praying but your Spirit interceding through me (316).

• Spend much time with God's Word.

Before opening God's Word, ask the Holy Spirit to enlighten your mind. In every verse the Holy Spirit will speak. His messages through the Word are as personal as if you heard an audible voice.

This topic offers much to explore! Consider these options:

**Application**

- Use a concordance and look up a few of the entries under "Holy Spirit" (in the KJV concordance look under "Holy Ghost").
- Turn to the index in books such as *The Desire of Ages,* or *Messages to Young People,* and look up some of the references under "Holy Spirit." Copy down two or three sentences that you like best, as subject matter for prayer.
- Do the same with *Testimonies for the Church.* All but volume 2 have entries under "The Holy Spirit," with volumes 5-9 especially rich.

# 30

# Pray "More and More" Like Jesus

**"We are transformed in ever-increasing splendour into his own image, this is the work of the Lord who is the Spirit" (2 Corinthians 3:18, Phillips).**

"By beholding we become changed." Phillips translation, in the King James, and in almost every other version those five words summarize the above statement of Paul to the Corinthians. Let's say it again: *By beholding we become changed.* Transformed! And as you behold Jesus, your love for Him "abound[s] still more and more" (Philippians 1:9) The Spirit helps as you seek to live the way the previous chapter of this book suggests. Paul's prayer for the Philippians says something about the Spirit that I find tremendously encouraging, namely:

"Being filled with the fruits of righteousness which are by Jesus Christ, to the glory and praise of God" (Philippians 1:11). *Being filled.* It's an ongoing experience.

**Your easy-to-love Savior**

*Cruden's Complete Concordance* lists about 140 names or titles for Jesus, one of which is *Teacher.* Under "Christ" in the *Comprehensive Index to the Writings of Ellen G. White,* one finds fifty topics, one of which is "Appellations of." One name in that section, "Educator and Teacher," has modified names such as the following:

- beloved Teacher and Friend
- best Teacher world has ever known
- humble Teacher of Galilee
- Master Teacher

- patient Teacher
- prince of Teachers

Counting modified names, one finds in the writings of Ellen White more than one thousand titles and appellations for our Savior! Like the above, each reveals something attractive about the character of Jesus. God has given remarkable pen pictures. From the chapter in *Education* titled "The Teacher Sent From God," here are a few glimpses of what Jesus was like as a Teacher:

- "Never was there another whose sympathies were so broad or so tender. A sharer in all the experiences of humanity, He could feel not only for, but with, every burdened and tempted and struggling one" (78).
- "In every human being, however fallen, He beheld a son of God, one who might be restored to the privilege of his divine relationship" (79).
- "Looking upon men in their suffering and degradation, Christ perceived ground for hope where appeared only despair and ruin. Wherever there existed a sense of need, there He saw opportunity for uplifting. Souls tempted, defeated, feeling themselves lost, ready to perish, He met, not with denunciation, but with blessing" (79).
- In every human being He discerned infinite possibilities. He saw men as they might be, transfigured by His grace. . . . Looking upon them with hope, He inspired hope. Meeting them with confidence, He inspired trust" (80).
- "Never before spoke one who had such power to awaken thought, to kindle aspiration, to arouse every capability of body, mind, and soul" (81).

**Abundant insights**

Do you recall my comments in the introduction about why I sometimes include Spirit of Prophecy comments? The above paragraphs illustrate the helpfulness of drawing insights from books like *Education.* And with the life of Jesus, *The Desire of Ages* helps make things personal. Jesus suffered for *me!* For *you!* For every person for whom you pray! On that cross *Jesus opened the gates of Paradise*—gates Satan can never, never close.

On page six we explained why we sometimes use the Spirit of Prophecy for insight and application. Since much of this book focuses on the Holy Spirit, reach out for His guidance continually. And know this: "God can do more in one moment by His Spirit than we can with our own labor in a lifetime" *(Manuscript Releases,* 21:208).

With the Holy Spirit's guidance and help, remember, too, the blood of Jesus. " ' "It is the blood that makes atonement for the soul" ' " (Leviticus 17:11). "The blood of Jesus is pleading with power and efficacy for those who are backslidden, for those who are rebellious, for those who sin against great light and love" (*Our High Calling,* 49).

**The certainty of victory**

When Moses wrote Leviticus, Calvary was still in the future. The fact that it's now history vastly increases the power of prayer. Note the wording of a verse about the great controversy: "Then I heard a loud voice saying in heaven, 'Now salvation, and strength, and the kingdom of our God, and the power of His Christ have come, for the accuser of our brethren, who accused them before our God day and night, has been cast down' " (Revelation 12:10).

What an assurance of victory! Here's what you can expect in your own life: "Those who feel the constraining love of God do not ask how little may be given in order to obtain the heavenly reward; they ask not for the lowest standard, but aim at a perfect conformity to the will of their Redeemer (*Testimonies for the Church,* 1:160).

God bless you as you pray for others, and as you seek more and still more of the Spirit's presence! And as you become still more and more like Jesus, of whom *In Heavenly Places* declares, "Prayer went before and sanctified every act of His ministry" (69).

**Application**

- "You were bought at a price" (1 Corinthians 6:20). As a comment on the price paid, the above source declares, "He gave all there was of Himself" (43). May you always do the same!

**If you enjoyed this book, you'll enjoy these other books by Joe Engelkemier as well:**

**30 Days to a More Powerful Prayer Life**

*Joe Engelkemier.* Find practical and essential ways to develop an undying prayer life in 30 days. This excellent book is applicable to relevant issues of today and was a valuable resource for NET '98.

0-8163-1648-1. Paperback. US$7.99, Cdn$11.99

**More and Still More**

*Joe Engelkemier.* Dig deeper into the spiritual treasure house of God. In this book, you will discover *more* joy than you can imagine, *more* prayer power than you can believe, *more* blessings than you can handle, *More and Still More* of everything God offers.

0-8163-1710-0. Paperback. US$4.97, Cdn$7.47.

**Great Prayers and Pray-ers of the Bible**

*Joe Engelkemier.* Through the examples of Job, Moses, Hannah, Elijah, Hezekiah, Jesus, and others, Joe helps us discover how to walk with God—on our knees—praying prayers of despair, supplication, triumph, reformation, and submission.

0-8163-1804-2. Paperback. US$8.99, Cdn$13.49

Order from your ABC by calling **1-800-765-6955**, or get online and shop our virtual store at **<www.adventistbookcenter.com>.**

- Read a chapter from your favorite book
- Order online
- Sign up for email notices on new products

Prices and availability subject to change.